The Book On GRATITUDE

*Abby —
great to meet you!
Keep sharing fun.
Jamie Sue Johnson*

JAN FRASER INSPIRED LIFE SERIES

The Book On
GRATITUDE

WRITTEN BY
30 International Women Authors

Foreword by Jack Canfield, co-creator of Chicken Soup for the Soul® and co-author of The Success Principles™

First Edition

Copyright ©2022 Jan Fraser Inspired Life Series
www.janfraser.com

All rights reserved.

ISBN: 979-8-9862809-5-0

No part of this book may be reproduced or transmitted in any form or by any means, electronic or mechanical, including photocopying, recording or by an information storage and retrieval system now known or hereafter invented — except by a reviewer who may quote brief passages in a review to be printed in magazine, newspaper or on the Web — without permission in writing from the publisher.

Acknowledgements
Director of Book Production: Jennie Ritchie | www.jennieritchie.com
Book Designer: Sue Luehring | sjldesign.carbonmade.com
Website designer: Myrto Mangrioti | www.loving-living.com

www.bookongratitude.com

We dedicate this book to you . . . our readers, our sisters, friends, mothers, aunts, grandmothers, teachers, leaders and all the unsung heroes in our world who have made it a better place.

We thank you.

No matter your circumstance, your country, your story, we walk alongside each of you as we share gratitude for each other.

Healing the World with Gratitude

CONTRIBUTING AUTHORS

Regina Andler – *USA*
Joy Bach – *USA*
Barbara Blue – *Ireland*
Penny Bongato – *Phillipines*
Paddy Briggs – *Canada*
Beatriz Maria Centeno – *USA*
Victoria Chadderton – *USA*
Sina Ciampa – *Canada*
Gayle Dillon – *USA*
Maria Duffy – *Bermuda*
Ann Smith Gordon – *Bermuda*
Robin Eldridge Hain – *USA*
Helen Holton – *USA*
LouAnne Hunt – *Canada*
Trisha Jacobson – *USA*
Linda Rose Jensen – *USA*

Jamie Sue Johnson – *USA*
Lila M. Larson – *Canada*
Maria Elena Laufs – *Spain*
Myrto Mangrioti – *Greece*
Sarah McCalden – *England*
Diane & Bob Palmer – *USA*
Bernadette Ridge – *USA*
Jennie Ritchie – *USA*
Cindy Stewart – *USA*
Alaria Taylor – *USA*
Cherylanne Thomas – *USA*
KDB (Karmen De Bora)
Wheeler – *USA*
Jane Williams – *USA*
Ilka V. Wilson Vallee – *Panama*

Reprinted with Permissions

TABLE OF CONTENTS

Introduction
Jennie Ritchie...1

Foreword
Jack Canfield..5

Gratitude for Life
Jan Fraser...9

Featured Author
Shift to the Gift – Jamie Sue Johnson........................15

Feeling Gratitude
Thank You, Daddy – Alaria Taylor.............................24
The Magic of Intentionally
Raising Our Vibration – Trisha Jacobson......................33
What Me, Be Grateful? – Gayle Dillon.........................41
Choosing Gratitude – Penny Bongato...........................49
A Life of Gratitude – Ann Smith Gordon.......................53
Helping Me Live – Sarah McCalden.............................61
The Gratitude of Connection – Jane Williams..................67

Choosing Gratitude
For this, I am Grateful – Sina Ciampa........................75
Journaling is Overrated – Regina Andler......................81
Gratitude for Compassion – Beatriz Maria Centeno.............89
The Biggest Gift of My Life – Barbara Blue...................95
Magical Moments – Victoria Chadderton.......................101
The Discipline of Practicing Gratitude – Cherylanne Thomas....107

Inspiring Gratitude

When One Plus One is So Much More
Than Two – Robin Eldridge Hain 115
Gifts of Gratitude and Quiet Joy – Cindy Stewart. 121
Hardships and Blessings – Joy Bach. 127
Finding Gratitude in Trauma – KDB Wheeler. 135
Dad's Legacy – LouAnne Hunt. 143
There is Always Hope – Linda Rose Jensen 149
The Power of Leading with Gratitude – Ilka V. Wilson Vallee 157
Keep Going! – Maria Duffy 163

Sharing Gratitude

Gratitude is Timeless – Lila M. Larson. 171
Activating the Law of Attraction with Gratitude – Myrto Mangrioti . . 177
It's Never too Late – Paddy Briggs 185
Grateful Start = Grateful Heart – Diane & Bob Palmer 189
Take a Letter, Maria – Maria Elena Laufs 195
Gratitude for My Like Minded Tribe – Bernadette Ridge. 201
Resilience, Grace & Gratitude Saved My Life – Helen Holton. 209

Invitation 215

INTRODUCTION

My mom has always been my biggest cheerleader.

When I was in 7th grade and was bullied in the bathroom by a group of big girls because I was trying to help a fellow student, she was ready to march into the office and confront their parents.

When I met the man that would become my husband, she baked cookies with me and mailed them across the country to him.

When I had to drive cross-country multiple times for my husband's job, who was right there beside me in the passenger seat? My mom . . . with her favorite set of audio tapes and a yellow notepad full of to-dos and memories.

When I was teaching school full-time, she encouraged me to follow my passion and become a life coach, author, speaker, and trainer.

She has always believed in and encouraged me – but she hasn't only done that for me. She has encouraged strangers, groups of people from stages, her grandkids, authors in this book and thousands of others around the globe.

My mom is Jan Fraser, the creator of the Inspired Life Series. The series began in 2021 when the world was recovering from the effects of the international pandemic. The first book was *The Book on Joy*® followed by *The Book on Transformation*®. *The Book on Gratitude*® is the third best-selling book in the series.

It is only fitting to introduce this *Book on Gratitude* by expressing my gratitude for the amazing person she is. She is virtually self-made, from growing up as the shy youngest sister of three girls from hard-working parents to inspiring women from every walk of life. She has a dreamer's heart and doesn't know the word *'No'* . . . never giving stock to naysayers.

I am grateful for her love, vision, her *'Anything is possible'* attitude, her ability to see the best in people and her strength. (You'll gain a little insight by reading her story on page 11.)

She comes by it honestly, descending from a line of strong women and men who forged their way as citizens of this country, farmers, nurses, entrepreneurs, military men and laborers. When no one believed that Jan's mother, Sadie, could become a nurse, she worked her way through training and did it anyway because she felt it was her calling. Then, leaving behind the comforts of Ohio and her family, traveled by ship on New Year's Eve 1937 from San Francisco to Honolulu, Hawaii, where she met and married my grandfather. She survived the 1941 attack on Pearl Harbor.

For those of you who have not had this kind of influence from your mom, I pray that you have found it elsewhere, or will seek out a cheerleader to have in your corner...someone who believes in you and supports you in finding your purpose and happiness in life, no matter what that looks like.

Three of the most important concepts to my mom are family (natural or acquired), impact and legacy, which is why she has gathered 29 amazing authors from around the world to share their stories of gratitude with you. As we view the planet today, we see challenges that could benefit from increased gratitude shared globally.

It is our collective hope that the thoughts, words, and suggestions contained in these chapters will help you feel more gratitude, making your life happier, better and more joy filled.

This book is divided into four sections surrounding gratitude: Feeling, Choosing, Inspiring and Sharing.

In the **Feeling Gratitude** Section, you'll read about treasuring family members and dear friends, past and present, gratitude for a birth island, and learn how to feel more gratitude and grace. Also, you'll discover how a life was saved and those in recovery were supported. Authors in this section hail from the Philippines, UK, Bermuda, and the US.

In **Choosing Gratitude**, we are introduced to stories surrounding grief and loss of spouses, babies, parents, and family pets. Techniques for deciding to be grateful regardless of the situation with authors from Ireland, Canada and the US are shared.

Stories in the **Inspiring Gratitude** section remind us that inspiration can come from both within us or from someone else and deals with mental and physical health, leadership, and Olympic Gold. These authors are from Panama, Bermuda, Canada, and the US.

In the **Sharing Gratitude** section, we see how our authors have spread their messages of gratitude in coaching sessions, media, magazines, letters and one-on-one. These chapters deal with love, aging relatives, job loss, multiple surgeries and becoming a centerfold. The authors are from Canada, Greece, Spain, and the US.

Within these pages, my mom and the other authors hope you will find inspiration and strategies for feeling and expressing more gratitude in your life. We truly believe that gratitude can heal the world. We hope you not only enjoy this book, but as a result, have a desire to spread the gift of gratitude to those in your sphere/to those you meet.

> "Be thankful for what you have; you'll end up having more. If you concentrate on what you don't have, you will never, ever have enough." — Oprah Winfrey

Welcome to our *Inspired Life Series* Community!
With Gratitude and Love,

Jennie

Jennie Ritchie
Director of Book Production

Jack Canfield

Jack Canfield, known as America's #1 Success Coach, is a bestselling author, professional speaker, trainer, and entrepreneur. He is the founder and CEO of the Canfield Training Group, which trains entrepreneurs, educators, corporate leaders and motivated individuals how to accelerate the achievement of their personal and professional goals.

He has conducted live trainings for more than a million people in more than 50 countries around the world. He holds two Guinness World Record titles and is a member of the National Speakers Association's Speaker Hall of Fame.

Jack is the coauthor of more than two hundred books, including, *The Success Principles™: How to Get from Where You Are to Where You Want to Be, The Success Principles Workbook,* and the *Chicken Soup for the Soul®* series, which includes forty New York Times bestsellers and has sold more than 500 million copies in 47 languages around the world.

Jack is a featured teacher in the movie *The Secret*, and has appeared on more than a thousand radio and television shows, including *The Oprah Winfrey Show, Oprah's Super Soul Sunday, the Today show, Fox & Friends,* and *Larry King Live.*

Foreword

By Jack Canfield

Co-Creator of the best-selling *Chicken Soup for the Soul*® series
Co-Author of *The Success Principles*™

Gratitude is one of the three most important emotional states (along with love and joy) for creating and living a happy, successful and abundant life. And you now hold in your hands a powerful tool to help you expand your experience of gratitude. *The Book on Gratitude* is a veritable feast for anyone who may have given up on choosing an attitude of gratitude or has forgotten the magic power that being grateful for the simple little things as well as the big things in life has for creating a more joyful, loving, satisfying, meaningful and successful life.

In my forty years of work with the Law of Attraction, I know how powerful gratitude can be to help people manifest what they want in their lives. I am continually telling my students, trainers, and members of my speaking audiences that the more they focus on creating, embracing and expressing gratitude, the easier and more abundant their lives will become. So, when Jan approached me to write the foreword for *The Book on Gratitude*, I instantly said yes for three reasons.

First, I believe we need to create a lot more gratitude in our world. Over the last fifty years as a motivational and inspirational speaker and transformational trainer, I have emphasized the need to maintain a high vibrational state of gratitude while keeping one's dreams and goals in sight. Gratitude is a critical aspect of achieving those dreams and goals because when we are living in a state of gratitude, we attract more things to be grateful about.

Gratitude is a joyful and selfless expression of thankfulness from within. Whenever you are in a state of gratitude and appreciation, you are in a state of natural abundance. Through gratitude and appreciation, you are focusing your thoughts and energy on the beauty and abundance that is already present in your life. And you are sending a clear message to the universe that this is what you would like to experience more of. There is no greater prayer than one of sincere heartfelt gratitude, appreciation, and love.

With all the challenges we are facing in our current world, gratitude is deeply needed in our lives. As you'll discover as you read this book and practice expressing more gratitude in your life, gratitude is contagious. And we lift others up — our families, our friends and ultimately our larger communities — when we are in a state of gratitude. Along with love, gratitude has the power to relax, heal, soothe, and comfort us.

I want to strongly encourage you to make a conscious decision to have an attitude of gratitude. You can choose to live in a state of constant joy, gratitude, and appreciation, and acknowledge how fortunate you are. Don't take even the simplest things for granted—appreciate them and give thanks.

In the last three years I have been introduced to the power of essential oils. Utilizing Young Living's Gratitude essential oil blend (a blend of ten powerful essential oils) will assist you in more easily creating a consciousness of gratitude. I know because I use it, and I strongly encourage you to try it. There is a ton of research that affirms that feeling and then expressing gratitude is immensely beneficial for you. It increases your sense of well-being, enthusiasm, optimism, happiness, and determination. It's good for your health and your longevity. It raises your vibrational (emotional) frequency and thus creates an upward-spiraling process of ever-increasing joy, appreciation for life, and abundance that just keeps getting better and better.

My second reason for saying yes to writing this foreword is that Jan has identified thirty amazing women whose lives radiate gratitude, and encouraged them to share their heartfelt messages within these pages. The thirty heart-centered authors of this book are also graduates of my *Breakthrough to Success* and my *Train the Trainer* programs and are actively living the principles they'll be sharing with you. They know the magic ingredient in life is gratitude. They are a culturally diverse group of women from eight different countries and all are speakers, trainers, coaches, counselors, and mentors, and just like you, they have faced many challenges both personally and professionally in their lives. And they will be sharing powerful stories of how they have learned to move confidently and more gracefully through life facing whatever challenges and obstacles might appear with wisdom, strength, and gratitude.

Thirdly, the stories they share are all true, inspiring, and uplifting. Having co-authored and edited more than *200 Chicken Soup for the Soul®* books, which are read in more than fifty languages all around the world, bringing hope, courage, inspiration, and love to millions of people, I know how these types of stories of hope, intention, triumph and resiliency are an unquestionably powerful tool in helping to transform people's lives. As you read the stories in this book, I encourage you to allow them to touch you deeply, and then quickly apply what they are teaching you. If you do, then they can absolutely begin to change your life.

Finally, be grateful for everything that shows up in your life. One of the things I teach is that "what is in the way, is the way." The challenges and obstacles that appear along your path are all opportunities to develop and to grow. Perhaps you are being called to develop new qualities like compassion, forgiveness, courage, resilience, and perseverance. Perhaps you are being called to develop new behaviors like standing up for yourself, setting boundaries, saying no to other people's expectations, demands and requests, and boldly asking for what you want. Be grateful for all of life no matter how it shows up. Also, when you act from the belief that the universe has your back and is on your side, and that everything that happens is happening for you and not to you or against you, your life becomes very magical.

Jack Canfield

Jan Fraser

J an is a 'self-starter', bringing real world customer service experience to her keynotes, training and coaching. An airline industry superstar, she rose from the ramp support team to instructor, training thousands of flight attendants.

Jan was a Seminar Speaker for Skill Path and National Seminars, and Adjunct Professor at Bermuda College. She is a Success and Writing Coach and traveled the world to deliver training in the US and seven countries.

Jan is a sought after Keynote Speaker. She is the author of nine books and coaches writers through virtual and onsite retreats. She co-created the *Success University for Women* series and is the Creator of the Jan Fraser Inspired Life Series best sellers.

She has a CSP® (Certified Speaking Professional™) designation from the National Speakers Association.

Jan lives with her husband in Lake Las Vegas and Bermuda, balancing her life between two shores.

Contact
Website: www.janfraser.com
Email: jan@janfraser.com

Gratitude for Life

By Jan Fraser

"This is a wonderful day. I've never seen this one before."

— Maya Angelou

Every day creates new opportunities to experience gratitude and at 75 years of living, it's a perfect time for reflection.

It's waking up and knowing in your heart that a myriad of experiences awaits you that could bring a day of profound and deep meaning to your life.

I've realized that gratitude opportunities come to me in four ways: Daily, Dramatic, Difficult, Dynamic.

Daily Gratitude

Daily gratitude is an ongoing and constant choice. If I am aware and awake there will be times in my day to give *'daily gratitude'* or receive it from someone else. It could be as simple as a quick thank you to someone for holding the door open for you as you struggle into a shop with your arms full of packages.

Or it might be taking the time to greet someone who may not know anyone in that location or gathering and may be feeling alone.

A few years ago, we traveled to Zimbabwe. It was my first time on the African continent. I was absorbed in new experiences and felt the energy of the people and their intention to represent their country in the best possible light.

At our hotel every morning for breakfast, we were greeted by a friendly staff who made us feel completely welcome. One young waitress in the restaurant was radiant with a smile to light the world.

Her nametag read *'More Blessings.'* I felt that must be the English translation of her name and I was curious about it and her. I initiated a chat and asked her how she received that name.

She told me her mother was expecting her as the 9th child in the family and named her *'More Blessings'* as she would be the embodiment of her name. I loved the explanation and immediately bonded to *'More Blessings.'* Every day I looked for her at breakfast to share messages of love, hope and inspiration. I thought how wonderful for her to go through life knowing she was a joy to others. They would be grateful for knowing her and receiving her kindness and energy.

When I live in the *daily gratitude* zone, I feel better, kinder and more respectful of others.

It increases the joy quality of my life. When I see my gratitude message shared with another person, their face lights up and they feel appreciation warming their heart.

It's a *'win-win'* situation. We both experience more happiness in that moment.

Dramatic Gratitude

> *"In a universe that's an intelligent system with a divine creative force supporting it, there simply can be no accidents. As tough as it is to acknowledge, you had to go through what you went through in order to get to where you are today, and the evidence is that you did."* — Wayne Dyer

Dramatic Gratitude usually occurs when there is a sudden change in your life, oftentimes involving danger. The result is shocking.

It was a freezing cold night. I was returning to my hotel after a temporary work assignment via the busiest freeway in the state, I-75.

On that night, I encountered black ice for the first time. In an instant, my rental car spun around, and I was facing oncoming traffic traveling upwards of 70 miles per hour coming in my direction. I quickly and safely moved the car to the side of the road. In a flash of thought, I realized this is what causes 'multi-car' pileups and I would be the reason for it tonight.

I took a few minutes to compose myself and called my daughter 2500 miles away. I needed to feel grounded for my next maneuver and hear her voice. I was thankful she was home and answered on the first ring. I told her what had happened and that I was grateful to be off the freeway though still headed in the wrong direction. She was calming. I decided to wait however long it was necessary for the traffic to lessen allowing me to do a U-turn on the freeway and get the car going the right direction, hopefully without encountering more black ice or speeding cars.

I was successful that night in getting the car back on the freeway heading toward my hotel again. I spoke my gratitude loudly, fervently, and continuously. If you have ever experienced an escape of accidental proportions, I know you understand my intensity at that moment of *dramatic gratitude*.

That experience impacted my life with renewed caution, care and focus on the road though black ice was difficult to see until you were on it. Later that night, I researched how to avoid it and be more aware of the weather and road conditions that might cause it to appear.

The experience on that cold night in Ohio also encouraged me to have more gratitude for my family, my faith and quick thinking. It made me treasure my life more.

Difficult Gratitude

"There are only two days in the year that nothing can be done. One is called yesterday and the other is called tomorrow. So today is the right day to love, believe, do, and mostly live." — Dalai Lama

I was on the floor of the bathroom crying. The floor was hard but I didn't care. I didn't want my two precious young daughters to get involved in the conflict or try to protect me. It was the only safe place with a locking door for privacy. I had been slapped across the face and I needed to cry it out.

I did not want any sadness to fall into my daughters' lives because of me.

I hope you have not had a time or a moment where you were frightened, fearful and unsure of what your next move would be. If you have experienced something like this, I can relate. Protecting my girls was my main priority. I am sure you had a main priority as well.

He said, "I want you gone by Monday!"

I said, "Ok, I'm taking the girls with me."

At the time, I felt like my world was falling apart, and financially it was, as his job was steadier and more substantial than mine. I knew, somehow, I would make it to ensure the road to our next life would be positive. That was a difficult time for us.

Yet, even during the upheaval, I felt gratitude for our safety. We packed a few things, and I took the girls to stay at my parents who were luckily an hour's drive away. They took us in immediately and I began to plan our next steps as best I could without damaging the minds of my daughters.

I wanted them to continue at their schools so changes in their lives would be minimized.

My parents offered love and a safe harbor during our transitionary time. I came to realize the tremendous gratitude I felt for my parents and my sister who helped financially until I got back on my feet. It felt good to pay her back for her support.

I secured a higher paying job as a claims adjuster for a well-known insurance company. Though it was a man's world, construction and estimating damages and re-builds, I tackled the training head-on as our lives depended on it. And they did.

We were in a much healthier environment without all the negativity that we had endured. I secured a new place for us to live, and we prospered.

My gratitude was voiced daily for this opportunity to breathe easier and feel safe. The girls were successful at school and in the community. I was grateful that even though we had weathered a difficult time, we felt gratitude. It worked wonders for our joy and happiness to reflect on gratitude.

Dynamic Gratitude

> "What you think, you become, What you feel, you attract. What you imagine, you create." — Buddha

Wonders and miracles appear to us when we view the sunrise or sunset.

Nature is awe-inspiring. At times, life is moving so fast we have little chance to wrap our arms around the universe and give thanks for all that we see and what is possible.

I have celebrated at the birth of my grandchildren.

I have even revived one of Enzi's (our German shepherd's) newborn puppies by giving it mouth-to-mouth resuscitation. My daughters witnessed it and were awestruck. I didn't know if it would work . . . and, miraculously, it did. All our puppies survived.

We breathe life into our relationships. We give thanks for all who are in our family, the one we are born into and the one we find and gather to us.

Gratitude softens the heart.

Gratitude is the balm that eases suffering, celebrates humanity, and brings joy and happiness.

Gratitude expressed comes back to us tenfold.

Let's share and Heal the World with Gratitude!

Gratitude Opportunities

- Give gratitude for at least one person a day.
- Pause for a few moments daily to express the Gratitude that is in your heart or on your mind.
- Keep a Gratitude Journal where you can write three things you are grateful for at the end of the day.
- Go outside once a day to lift your arms into the air and breathe deeply while you express your Gratitude for all you see and that You Can See.

Jamie Sue Johnson

Jamie Sue's life has been her classroom. She has spent years on her own personal journey: in business, transformation, and leadership. She has studied under many leaders in the industry. Not only has she been a Transformational Leadership Coach, Keynote Speaker and Trainer for over 24 years, to add to her credentials, she is a Laughter Yoga Facilitator and is trained in Jack Canfield's Success Principles. She leads experiential keynotes, workshops and retreats. She invented the LIVE IT! Life Series. Where you: Dream it. Design it. Do it.

Jamie Sue enjoys living in the Orlando, Florida area, where she loves sharing time with her family, friends and travels with her Ski Club. As a member of LIONS Club International she has raised scholarships for students at The Ohio State School for the Blind, and she supports the SIDS Foundation.

Are you ready for your best life to come to life? Dream it. Design it. Do it. Let's Live it!

Contact
Website: www.jamiesuejohnson.com
Email: jamiesue@jamiesuejohnson.com

Shift to the Gift

By Jamie Sue Johnson

"Be in a state of gratitude for everything that shows up in your life. Be thankful for the storms as well as the smooth sailing."

— Wayne Dyer

I wrapped my arms around my daughter's daycare sitter as we huddled in the back seat of a police car. We were heading to the Emergency Room at Stanford where my younger daughter, Sarah, had been taken by ambulance minutes before. On arrival, another police officer greeted us. I grabbed him by his neck, pulled him down closely, looked him directly in the eyes and spoke, "She (pointing to our sitter) did everything right, please take great care of her. I must go now," as I raced to the Emergency Room entrance.

A case worker escorted me to a private room where I immediately called Sarah's father at work to let him know we were in the Emergency Room at Stanford Children's Hospital. Sarah had stopped breathing.

I hung up the phone, got down on my knees, and prayed. Asking God to step in. I was scared to the core.

After what seemed like forever, the case worker came and took me to Sarah's bedside. There were tubes and hoses everywhere and she was on a ventilator. This nine-week-old baby girl had been resuscitated but was not breathing on her own.

I slowly turned to see members of the ER staff, the EMTs, Paramedics, Fire Fighters and the Police Officers that had tended to my daughter's care. I looked at each and every set of their eyes and thanked each of them for taking Care of Sarah. I nodded in gratitude for their service to my daughter.

Later that afternoon, when we were told that Sarah was not stable and had no reflexes, we were devastated.

In desperation, to find a golden nugget, I asked if we could donate her organs? I thought that if we could donate her organs, we could give lasting meaning to her life.

The doctor shared with us that, had they known what happened, like a car accident or a drowning — the why and when she stopped breathing, then they would have known how long her organs had gone without oxygen. Since they did not know the cause, organ donation was not an option.

I thought . . . Really GOD?! What is the point of this? This nine-week-old tiny person being moved to Angel status. It cannot be happening, right?

Do you recall a show on CBS called "Touched by an Angel"? Monica, Tess, and Andrew were the main Angel characters. The premise was that Angels were sent to support you when you were in a troubling situation. They were there to give you hope and to reassure your faith. Even if things didn't turn out the way you had hoped, there was always a feeling of an angel's touch and a loving message.

Reflecting on "Touched by an Angel" TV show, I asked aloud, "Where are Andrew, Monica and Tess?" If those angels weren't here with us right now then Sarah wasn't meant to die. I know it's a bit crazy, and I had to think of something else other than this tragedy. "Touched by an Angel" spurred a positive set of thoughts that I grasped onto to lighten the mood. An angel's touch to ease the pain.

Later that day after Sarah had been moved to the ICU, the Emergency Room doctor came to follow up. When he entered the room, he had to turn away to wipe the tears from his eyes. I reached out and touched his shoulder. He shared that the neurology reports were not promising. She had lost significant brain function and was not able to breathe on her own. She would not be able to survive without massive medical intervention.

I called my mother, father and sister to let them know Sarah was in critical condition and may not make it through the night. They planned to arrive the next day.

My older daughter arrived at the hospital and said goodbye to Sarah. Our wonderful neighbors took my big girl home, so we could stay with the baby. So grateful for the support from friends and neighbors.

As a final measure to make sure nothing was missed, we requested the Neurologist complete the battery of tests once again before we made a decision regarding life support. He returned at 10 PM that night and the prognosis was still the same. "Significant brain damage. Sarah would never eat or breathe on her own."

Angels started arriving. My cousin, our minister, and our close friends gathered at the hospital to support us.

We prayed, reviewed the options and facts, and discussed our feelings. We asked what kind of life would she have in a hospital bed? We chose to take Sarah off life support.

The nurses removed the tubes and hoses, and the machines stopped. Nestled in a corner, I held my baby as we sat in the rocking chair supported by my Angels. I was grateful for Sarah's father, my cousin, and our minister. I wrestled with all the blankets to find Sarah's foot to hold onto.

As I rocked and held her,
Sarah took her
last,
few,
breaths . . .

I could hardly move. I asked her father what was next. He asked me to give her to him. He laid her on the hospital bed and covered her with her blanket. We all stepped out of the room so the nurses could attend to Sarah.

A storm we shall definitely never forget.

A few days after Sarah transitioned to Angel status, the police called to ask if two officers could come by the house. I said, "Sure, of course!" When they arrived, my family and close friends were seated around the dining room table and the knock came on the door.

I opened the door and invited in the two policemen from the Palo Alto Police Department. They held a most beautiful bouquet of flowers and cards signed from them and all the EMTs, Emergency Room staff, and Firefighters.

These police officers were the same two that arrived at the scene when our sitter had to call 911. One that drove us to the Emergency Room, and the other who I had left with our sitter when we arrived at the ER.

With tears in their eyes, they thanked me . . . me! They thanked me for who I was and how I acted during the tragic affair. They acknowledged me! I was deeply touched by their sympathy and heartfelt care. My family, friends and I could not thank them enough for their great service to Sarah and their lovely gifts of sympathy.

Trying to make sense of this storm over the next few weeks and months, I started to see the miracles that occurred after Sarah's death, and this assisted me to 'shift to the gift' of Sarah's tragic passing and to find the golden nuggets that gave me the strength to get through.

Where in your life have you had something horrific, tragic, or just plain upsetting happen? Can you see for yourself where you might still be suffering over an event, a situation, a loss? Is it holding you from healing?

Here are ways I moved through the healing process and am now able to 'shift to the gift.'

First, I have always written in a journal. Journaling allows a safe space to get it all out. All the raw emotions, feelings, anger, bargaining, denial, and depression and 'goofy-ness,' too!

Next, I attended a neo-natal death support group and worked with other families that were impacted by losing a child. I was very blessed at that time to be part of a transformational leadership program through Landmark Education, where my colleagues and the leaders were available to me to assist me.

During the months that followed, I received a copy Chicken Soup for the Soul. I found a story in the chapter On Death and Dying written by Sara Parker, entitled 'She Was Waiting.' I tore the chapter out of the book and kept it in my journal to remind me of the "plan" greater than myself and "all in God's time." I read this story every year in honor of Sarah as I celebrate her birthday and death day. I love flowers, so I buy myself white roses every year.

And even today, yes even today, when I have a thought or a feeling and notice I am suffering over the loss of Sarah, I ask myself these questions.

1. Is there something that I need to feel and process? If so, I allow the feelings to wash over me, but not wallow in them. Then, I pick up my journal to get it all out.
2. Is there something I need to say and to whom? Then, I make that communication happen. Just so you know, God was on that list a number of times.
3. Could I be playing the victim of 'not good enough"? If yes to this one, that is when I know I need to make the shift to being grateful for the many blessings that have come from this for me. Suffering, Settling and Surviving is optional. We really do have a choice.
4. What can I be grateful for? Even something small can support you to start to move through what you may be feeling.

This process has served me very well over these many years since Sarah's passing.

The biggest and best gift that came out of Sarah's passing, I declare is, I have Sarah to thank for the journey that has led me straight to you today. You see, the fall after Sarah passed, I created my Life Coaching and Executive Coaching firm. I started training people to become coaches and became a part of the leadership team with Accomplishment Coaching. I have developed the Live It! Life Series. Through my work, I have been able to support many folks to learn how to "Shift to the Gift" in life's storms and find the golden nuggets, silver linings and the rainbows after the storms.

I am thankful for all the love and support we received during that tragic time. And today, I want to do a special shout out to all our Police, Firefighters, EMTs and Health Care Professionals as they need our love and support now more than ever.

Now these many thousands of miles away and many years after that storm at Children's Hospital, when I am dining out and I notice Police Officers, EMTs, Firefighters or Health Care Professionals, I anonymously pick up their check. I ask the server to say to them, "The party that picked up your check today wanted me to share with you this message. 'Thank you for the gift you are to our community and giving your Angel's touch to our world. Please remember that you make a difference each and every day.'"

So, my gratitude challenge for you, if you will accept it is: The next time you see a Police Officer, EMT, Firefighter or Health Care Professional in the grocery store, at a corner, or at a restaurant give them a wave and a thank you or pick up their check! You, too, can make a difference when you add your Angel's touch.

I will be forever grateful to our friends and families, the students, families and teachers at El Carmelo Elementary School, my coworkers at CBT Systems, Lucile Packard Children's Hospital Stanford staff, and the Palo Alto Police and Fire Departments for all their service and support during that tragic storm.

Life is what happens when you are planning something else. Shift to the Gift, and Live it!

Notes

JAN FRASER INSPIRED LIFE SERIES

Feeling

GRATITUDE

Alaria Taylor

Alaria Taylor is an award-winning singer-songwriter with over 50 national and regional awards. She has performed in almost every situation imaginable including cruise ships, coffeehouses, opera companies, with the Milwaukee Symphony, at Summerfest: The World's Biggest Music Festival, dinner theaters, clubs, on television and radio, and as the director of Chick Singer Night Milwaukee.

She was the co-owner and business manager of a successful holistic healthcare clinic for 36 years and the Consultant of the Year three years in a row with an international network marketing company. She is a Certified Jack Canfield Success Coach (all three levels), has degrees in psychology and counseling, and is a member of Mensa. She has been happily married to her husband Jeff, for over 36 years. She is a Success Coach/Consultant for individuals, groups, and businesses, as well as a vocal coach, helping people get from where they are . . . to where they want to be.

Contact

Websites:
www.alariataylorconsulting.com
www.alariataylor.com

Thank You, Daddy

By Alaria Taylor

"Be thankful for the small moments, both the hardships and the triumphs, for one day you'll look back and realize they were the very things that shaped your identity and made you who you are."

— Alaria Taylor

"I can see your underpants! I can see your underpants!" a swarm of sassy boys yelled up at me from 20 feet below. I was in grade school gym class, climbing a thick rope to the top of the two-story gymnasium where I was supposed to touch the ceiling and then climb back down. With just two of these giant ropes in the gym, only two kids climbed at a time. That meant the rest of the class remained at the bottom of the ropes looking upwards. Climbing this rope was terrifying enough without being heckled from below by little boys with boy germs. I wanted to reach back and pull my dress tight to my legs, but that would mean plummeting to my death. Life is full of choices. And so, I continued to climb and the boys continued to shout.

At my grade school, girls were not allowed to wear pants. We could only wear dresses. We could bring snow pants or pants to wear at recess, but we had to put them on under our dresses and take them off at the back of the classroom in front of everyone — before and after every recess. As we would pull the pants up under our dresses, the boys would watch for a glimpse of our underpants. Then they would shriek, "I can see your underpants!" This happened multiple times a day, but for some reason, the rope climbing indignity was the final straw for me.

I was telling my dad about this humiliating situation at dinner one night. He said, "Well, why don't you do something about it?" I said, "What can I do? I'm 10 years old. It's the rule. We aren't allowed to wear pants." He suggested making a petition and then going to speak with the principal about it. I stopped in mid-bite and thought about it. Could this possibly work? I decided to try it. So, I wrote on a piece of notebook paper, "We the undersigned think that girls should be allowed to wear pants at school." I got right to the point without a lot of legal jargon. I took my petition out on the playground at recess and collected signatures from as many kids as I could. Almost everyone signed it, including the boys!

After school, I went to the office and in my most adult voice asked to speak to the principal. I wasn't sure he'd agree to see me. I was alone. My dad didn't fix this for me or go with me. He just made the suggestion and let me do it myself. The principal agreed to see me, ushered me into his office, and pointed for me to sit in the big chair across from his desk. I presented my case, told him about the utter humiliation we girls had been suffering because of this outdated rule, and then I showed him the petition. To my absolute surprise, he agreed with me and changed the rule on the spot! I was stunned. It worked! The feeling that rushed over me might be described as 'drunk with power.'

If I could do this, what else could I do?

From that day forward, girls were allowed to wear pants at Hales Corners Elementary School. This experience had a huge impact on me. I'm grateful to my father for suggesting I take action rather than just complain. I thought it was an impossible situation, the rules were the rules, and I was just a helpless kid. With a simple comment at the dinner table my dad taught me that I could make a difference and actually get a rule changed that had literally been in place since 1844, when the first school was built in Hales Corners (information courtesy of the Hales Corners Historical Society).

This was an empowering moment that stuck with me over the years. Thank you, Daddy.

As a Certified Jack Canfield Success Coach, I coach people and lead workshops using Jack's Success Principles as a guide. Jack's Poker Chip Theory of Self-Esteem teaches that taking risks builds your confidence. Every time you take a risk and succeed, it's like adding poker chips to your self-esteem account. The more poker chips you have, the more risks you'll feel comfortable taking in the future. You will play the game of life with confidence, because you have plenty of poker chips. This incident gave me a pile of poker chips that would serve me well in the future.

Anything is Possible

When I was about 9 years old, after reading several presidential biographies, I walked out into the family room and announced to my dad, "I want to be president of the United States." Looking up from his paper, he didn't laugh, snicker, or dismiss me. He calmly advised, "Well, you probably should go to law school, then run for Congress, and then maybe the Senate. After that, you'd be in position to run for president."

I said, "Thank you," turned around, and went back to my room to finish my book. He didn't mention that no woman had ever been president, or tell me it might be impossible. He remained completely serious and actually gave solid advice. I quickly moved on to other hopes and dreams for my future, but looking back, I am amazed my dad was able to keep a straight face.

I am forever grateful to my dad for not ridiculing my request, helping me believe anything was possible, and adding a few more poker chips to my account. Thank you, Daddy.

Never Give Up, Even When it Seems Impossible

It was early September, the day before cheerleading tryouts my freshman year in high school. I had spent every day after school for two weeks learning our high school fight song cheer and all the other required elements for tryouts. To say this was extremely important to me would be an understatement. The day before tryouts, I injured my leg playing soccer in gym class, severely spraining and straining my ankle and knee to the point where I was unable to put any weight on that leg. My mom took me to the doctor who said I had to stay on crutches for two weeks.

I was absolutely devastated. I had been a cheerleader in 8th grade and I loved it. In my mind, not being able to try out for the squad was a disaster of biblical proportions. I was crying and complaining to my dad at dinner, sobbing that everything was ruined, it wasn't fair, why did this have to happen the day before tryouts? He said, "Why don't you try out anyway?" I stopped chewing my pizza. What? Was that possible? Could I do this on one leg?

I hobbled on crutches to my bedroom to see if I could do all the required elements on one leg. First, the school fight song cheer. No problem. Whoa. Feeling a little more hopeful, I tried the jumps. The most difficult one in my situation was the stag jump, which involved crouching all the way down to the ground, then leaping in the air with one leg pointed backwards, the other bent forward, landing back down on the ground, then jumping up and standing at attention. It would be tricky doing this on one leg. I used my immobile leg as the straight leg since I couldn't bend that one. I now realize how difficult that was. It was like a pistol squat, but somehow, I was able to do it. I went to bed a little hopeful that night, instead of crying my eyes out.

The next day, after school, I nervously clomped on my crutches into the gym for tryouts. There were about 85 girls trying out for 5 spots. Several girls asked why I was there. I said I was still going to try out. Lots of raised eyebrows. Three teachers judged us as we got up one at a time to do the cheer, four jumps, splits, cartwheel, and other optional gymnastic tricks. One of the judges, a basketball coach, had a huge smile on his face during my turn. They announced the winners and I made the squad! I couldn't believe it!

The next day, my locker was plastered with signs from the older cheerleaders congratulating me. Upper classmen were pointing at me saying, "She's the one that made the cheerleading squad on one leg!" It was quite a splashy beginning to my freshman year in high school. Some of the girls were mad at me for being selected, but that's another story for another day. Making the squad that year impacted my life. First of all, it gave me confidence and taught me to never give up. Secondly, it influenced the friends and boyfriend I would have the next four years. I am still friends today with many from that group and actually married one of the boys I cheered for back then. We've been happily married for 36 years.

If my dad had not suggested trying out on one leg, it never would have occurred to me. I wouldn't have even tried and my life might have taken a different path. Once again, per the Jack Canfield Poker Chip theory of self-esteem...this event put more chips in my account. I not only gained a lot of self-confidence, but a strong belief that's it's never over, even when it seems impossible.

I am grateful to my dad for encouraging me to try out even when the odds seemed totally stacked against me. Thank you, Daddy.

Full Circle Moment — Anything is Possible

Summerfest: The World's Biggest Music Festival is in my hometown, Milwaukee, Wisconsin. It's in the *Guinness Book of World Records* as the most highly attended music festival in the world. My dad, a musician in a very popular band, was the first to play on the new Miller Jazz Oasis stage at Summerfest. I was just a little girl, but my dad took me along and I got to stand backstage watching him play in front of thousands of people. That moment remained etched in my mind all my life.

It all came full circle in 2007 when I was standing in that same spot on the same Miller Stage getting ready to sing for Summerfest's 40th Anniversary opening ceremonies. I had a friend take a picture of me standing where I stood decades earlier watching my dad. It was an amazing full circle moment and I was filled with gratitude during the entire day. Just before I walked on stage, the band that played before us was coming off and who did I meet in person for the very first time? Joy Bach, also an author in this book, who became a friend and we have sung together many times at 'Chick Singer Night Milwaukee' and at 'Best of Chick Singer Night' shows at Summerfest.

I am filled with gratitude for all of it. Filled with gratitude my dad took me with him that day to watch his band play. Filled with gratitude I got the chance to perform on the same stage. I'm even filled with gratitude for the so-called bad as well as the good. In the future, I would have many events far worse than boys yelling at me in grade school or injuring my leg the day before tryouts. These small victories gave me the poker chips to handle much more extreme adversity in my future. I'm filled with gratitude for all the lessons my dad taught me, even when he didn't realize he was teaching.

Those events impacted my life, added poker chips to my self-esteem account, and made me who I am today. Thank you, Daddy.

THE BOOK ON GRATITUDE

Notes

Trisha Jacobson

Trisha Jacobson is passionately committed to helping people breakthrough fear, overcome blocks and heed the intuitive whispers and heart's wisdom along the path to self-discovery.

She is an intuitive and compassionate teacher, a certified success principles trainer and best selling author who engages her readers, audiences and coaching clients; teaching conscious, subconscious and heart-centered tools to raise confidence, connect with purpose and create results that lead to more joy, happiness, success and fulfillment.

She is also the founder and owner of Ripple on Silver Lake, a wonderful, heart centered retreat center nestled in the beautiful lakes region and White Mountains of New Hampshire.

Contact

Websites: www.trishajacobson.com or www.rippleonsilverlake.com

The Magic of Intentionally Raising Our Vibration

By Trisha Jacobson

"Give yourself a gift of five minutes of contemplation in awe of everything you see around you. Go outside and turn your attention to the many miracles around you. This five-minute-a-day regimen of appreciation and gratitude will help you to focus your life in awe."

— Wayne Dyer

A teacher and mentor of mine once suggested that I live my life in a series of 30-day experiments. After giving it a try, I've discovered it's a wonderful way to try out a new way of thinking, develop a new habit or help us decide if we even want to commit to a daily practice. In my experience, making a simple 30-day commitment has helped me increase my water intake, got me into the habit of taking daily vitamin supplements and has helped me develop a new daily practice.

Lately, I've been feeling scattered. A short trip to Florida to see my 86-year-old Dad for a week turned into a rather challenging experience. After a wonderful visit, we were getting ready to head to the airport for my return flight. I was on the porch enjoying a wonderful sunrise. Dad was in his bedroom having a stroke. The stroke earned him an ambulance ride, a seven-day hospital stay, a fourteen-day admission to rehab and a six-week home care plan that made it impossible for him to be alone. In an instant, my short visit got extended to over a month and sent my family into crisis mode.

Adult children supporting aging parents know all about crisis mode. A single event can quickly alter best laid plans and be challenging for all involved. We are busy and living full lives with work, family and home responsibilities. Becoming a sudden caregiver in response to a clinical emergency can certainly disrupt the plan!

I own a lodging property and retreat center in the beautiful White Mountains of New Hampshire. Owning a historic retreat center on a lake in the mountains sounds wonderful to many, and it truly is, but there is certainly a lot involved in maintaining a circa 1903 property and running it as a profitable business. One thing I've learned about being a solo entrepreneur; if I'm not actively doing the work or coordinating the work, the work doesn't get done and the bills don't get paid.

It was April. I was in Florida caring for Dad and the summer season was fast approaching. Instead of getting the property ready for guests, I was 1100 miles away consumed with hospital visits and coordinating care plans with nurses, doctors, social workers, physical therapists, occupational therapists, and rehabilitation facilities. When I wasn't chasing down health care providers or dealing with paperwork, I was taking care of whatever my Dad needed to get through the frustration he had being trapped in bed and unable to do much of anything but wait.

As the days ticked by, my anxiety level increased. COVID had caused me major financial challenges and this was going to be the season that would make or break my lodging business. I needed to return to New Hampshire to my pre-season To Do List. I needed help! Asking for help has never been my strong point. I'm the oldest, the only girl and the only health care professional in the family, so as my parents aged and health issues arose, I was naturally the one who answered phone calls, coordinated their care and hopped on a plane to manage a crisis. But this time, I really needed help.

THE BOOK ON GRATITUDE

I contacted my three brothers to take my place as Dad needed support once he was discharged from rehab. I was relieved when they each committed to stay with Dad for a couple of weeks when he came home. My brother, Keith, was the first to arrive.

Fifteen minutes after getting home, Dad had an episode that returned him to the emergency room and hospital admission with more tests, rehab and follow-up appointments.

It took everything I had not to jump on a plane back to Florida and let everything back home go for another summer, which more than likely would have meant letting go of my property forever. Instead, I asked for help again. I asked my brothers to pitch in more time to cover Dad's new eight-week rehabilitation period so I could stay home, take care of business and monetize my summer and fall rental seasons.

I remember breathing a big sigh of relief and feeling an immense wave of gratitude come over me when my brothers agreed to cover for me. I could feel the stress flow out of my body as I looked over my To Do list. I slept peacefully for the first time in a long time, knowing I was off Dad duty.

The next morning, I woke up with a plan. I got dressed, put my coffee in a to-go cup and drove to the top of Cathedral Ledge. It was there on the top of that tall granite ledge, overlooking the spectacular view of the White Mountains, Echo Lake and the Mount Washington Valley that I remembered the Rampage of Uncommon Appreciation activity that my mentor told me about. In that moment, I committed to the practice for a 30-day Experiment.

Today, and every day for the past several weeks, I make coffee, pour it in my favorite mug, head out to a sunny spot on the deck and sit in my favorite chair with Sundae, my cat, purring at my feet. In this state, I close my eyes, take a few deep breaths and begin my new morning ritual of practicing uncommon appreciation. It certainly beats waking up to the news or my email box or my social media feed.

Once I've taken a few deep breaths, establishing a rhythm, to the count of three and out to the count of six, I bring into my awareness something I am grateful for. Sundae is my go-to if nothing else immediately comes to mind.

I imagine my heart expanding in my chest as I focus on just one thing I'm grateful for.

And then I dig a little deeper.

I relish the first sip of coffee. I immerse myself in the feeling of the morning air on my skin and the slight breeze or the sun shining on my face.

I listen to the sounds: birdsong, the buzz of cicadas, the leaves rustling in the breeze, the rooster cock-a-doodle-dooing in the distance, and Sundae purring next to me and the feeling of her fur when she stretches and rubs against my skin.

I open my eyes and look out over my yard. The farm off in the distance, the view of Mount Chocorua from the deck, the brook that runs along the border of my property, the garden that needs tending, the tall grass near the brook that needs mowing.

Wait! Stop! No adding things to my To Do list! All I need to do right now is simply breathe and focus on feeling uncommon appreciation.

I take a deep breath. I feel the chair supporting me. I reflect on the chair, the wood and the oak tree that supplied the wood and the craftsman who built this wonderfully comfortable rocking chair. My attention moves to the delivery truck, the driver and the infrastructure that delivered it and set it up on my deck. If I keep going, I can express gratitude for the gas station that fueled the truck, the food that nourished the driver while he traveled across the country. I could go on and on.

My attention moves to the pot of flowers. The lovely pink blossoms that attracted the hummingbird. I imagine the plant's origin and express gratitude for everything that brought this plant to my deck. I go deeper and imagine the seed in the greenhouse. My attention moves to the garden shop where I bought it and the family that works so hard to make sure that they have everything I need to enjoy my flowers every summer.

My attention shifts to the large tree in the yard. When it got struck by lightning, I thought it would die. Instead, it sent off a young shoot that is quite well established and provides wonderful shade for the hammock.

Oh, wait, there I go again, naturally trying to add things to my To

THE BOOK ON GRATITUDE

Do List. I remind myself to stay immersed in my Rampage of Uncommon Appreciation for a little bit longer.

The grass is so green this morning. There are at least 100 shades of green I can see from where I am sitting: natural greens from the national forest, grasses and other green vegetation in the hay field and the bank of the brook, the green leaves, the pine trees, and manicured green lawn. I am grateful for the man that rigged up an irrigation system that uses the water from the brook which got replenished during last night's rain.

I could go on and on.

My attention drifts back to my coffee cup, and I'm grateful for the miracle machine that brews it easily and tidy for me. My thoughts drift to a friend who despises the pods and the impact they have on the environment.

Wait. Stop. Back to gratitude and appreciation!

For me, I fully appreciate these pods that I use for my first cup of coffee each day and the simplicity they offer me so early in the morning. Later, when I am more awake and the work day begins, I'll switch over to the coffee pot. But not now. For now, I love the simplicity of this ritual with the pod that fills my cup and provides me with that wonderful first sip during my Rampage of Uncommon Appreciation.

I take another sip and reach down to pet Sundae. Her purr gets louder and her fur is so soft since I've been feeding her the new food the veterinarian suggested.

So, you see, this Rampage of Appreciation might never end. There is so much to be grateful for all around us and allowing ourselves to go deeper into a Rampage of Uncommon Appreciation for just a few minutes a day is a powerful habit to build.

Now, that it is a habit I've incorporated into my daily practice, I find myself doing it intentionally throughout the day to raise my vibration in any given moment.

For example, the other day, I found myself getting frustrated with the long line at the grocery store. Instead of allowing my frustration to grow, I simply picked something in my cart and followed it to its origin and to all that was involved in it getting into my cart. I chose

Sundae's new bag of cat food. I'm grateful for my phone that was able to take a picture of the cat food label so I would recognize it when I got to the store. I thought about the plant and the workers who manufacture it, ship it and stock it on the shelf so I could buy it. My attention shifted to the cashier who would soon ring me up, her supervisor who hired her (she is so pleasant).

I have noticed that, when I am in the space of gratitude, magical things happen and my days flow much easier. Sometimes I don't feel grateful, so I simply focus on my breath. Before long I find myself slipping into a Rampage of Appreciation around my breath, and how breathing delivers oxygen to all the cells of my body so each cell can do what it does to support me through my day.

My morning Rampage of Uncommon Appreciation is turning on a switch in my mind to access the magic of Universal flow.

I invite you to give it a try. Just 5-10 minutes a day. Be sure to have something to write with to capture any insights, inspiration, or actionable ideas this powerful practice of gratitude brings to you. ✸

THE BOOK ON GRATITUDE

Notes

Gayle Dillon

---※---

In the last twenty years, Rev. Gayle Dillon has become an Ordained Science of Mind Minister, Certified Canfield Trainer, Certified Oola Life Coach, International Coaching Federation trained coach and a person in recovery who believes we all can change our lives if we choose. Her life's passion is empowering people to reclaim their power over addiction. Her focus is to engage anyone interested in transforming their lives by taking responsibility for their choices and making a commitment to themselves to live an authentic, joyful life. Gayle is an inspiring speaker, motivating teacher, empowering coach, stimulating writer, compassionate leader, and thought-provoking ceremony officiant.

In answering an inner calling to live by the Pacific Ocean, Gayle and her husband Paul moved to Long Beach, WA with their dog, Gibson. Spirit didn't waste any time in making that dream a reality in her life and she now lives happily only a short walk through the dunes to the beach.

Contact
Website: www.messedup2blessedup.org
Email: revgayle@messedup2belssedup.org

What Me, Be Grateful?

By Gayle Dillon

"As we express our gratitude, we must never forget that the highest appreciation is not to utter words, but to live by them."

—John F. Kennedy

Our experiences form our life. I remember the first time I heard about a gratitude practice. In the Spring of 1989, I was arrested for having an illegal substance. After my court appearance, they gave me the option of treatment. While at the outpatient treatment center the counselor recommended, I start a gratitude practice.

You can imagine my response. 'What on earth do I have to be grateful for?' I got arrested. I'm at this treatment center. She told me I had choices, and I chose the treatment center. She listed my options: 1) treatment center, 2) jail (I argued this wasn't an option), 3) leave the state with no forwarding address (again, I argued this wasn't an option). She reminded me that even though I didn't see 2 and 3 as options, people chose them all the time. I begrudgingly began a gratitude practice. It was an introduction, not yet, a life style.

In 2002, the importance of gratitude resurfaced when I walked into a Religious Science Church for the very first time. The minister there (now my mentor, colleague, and friend) said to me "You are going to love these teachings. You get to take 100% responsibility for your life. You are going to hate these teachings. You get to take 100% responsibility for your life."

I started practicing gratitude daily, and I watched how I changed, and so did my life.

In 2020, I became a Certified Canfield Trainer. In Jack Canfield's book, *The Success Principles* and in his training, he shared a formula he learned from Dr. Robert Resnick: E+R=O. The E stands for EVENTS. Events happen to all of us throughout our lives. We jump over the R (I'll get back to that) and focus on the O, the OUTCOME. We blame the event for the outcome we are experiencing. And yet, how many times have you heard of an event that has happened to a group of people and yet the outcome for each is not the same? Why? Because it's the R, our RESPONSE, to the event that determines our outcome.

Here is an example of the E+R=O from Jack Canfield's *The Success Principles* book on pages 7-8:

> "I remember living in Los Angeles during a terrible earthquake. Two days later, I watched as a CNN reporter interviewed people commuting to work. The earthquake had damaged one of the main freeways leading into the city. Traffic was at a standstill, and what was normally a 1-hour drive had become a 2- or 3-hour drive.
>
> The CNN reporter knocked on the window of one of the cars stuck in traffic and asked the driver how he was doing.
>
> He responded angrily, 'I hate California. First there were fires, then floods, and now an earthquake! No matter what time I leave in the morning, I'm going to be late for Work. This sucks!'
>
> Then the reporter knocked on the window of the car behind him and asked the second driver the same question. This driver was all smiles. He replied, "It's no problem. I left my house at five a.m. I don't think under the circumstances my boss can ask for more than that. I have lots of music and my Spanish-language lessons with me. I've got my cell phone. I have coffee in a thermos, my lunch — I even brought a book to read. So, I'm fine."

THE BOOK ON GRATITUDE

You may be wondering what gratitude has to do with all of this and the simple answer is EVERYTHING.

I could lament all the wrong responses I have made in my life. I could be grateful for waking up and realizing the choice was and always has been mine. My first lesson in living a life of gratitude was when I realized I couldn't change my past. I could only move forward and be grateful for the lessons I have learned.

I spent a big chunk of my life living in the outcome. I played the victim, *Why me?* card repeatedly. My life only got better when I took responsibility for my thoughts and actions and the biggest take away, I can have to every situation is to be grateful.

Trust me, I know, when you are knee deep in poo; it is difficult to be grateful. The Truth, however, is in knowing that the sooner you can be grateful, the sooner you can find your path out of any situation.

Have you heard the popular parable about the two young boys: one an optimist, one a pessimist?

I love this story: "Both boys were left alone in a room with a big pile of horse poo in the middle of the floor. It was a scientific experiment. They were both given shovels. The scientists left the room and when they came back a few hours later they noticed something amazing. One little boy had a scowl on his face and was sitting angrily with his back against a wall in the corner of the room. His arms were folded across his chest with his shovel sitting on the floor next to him. He yelled, 'WHY did you leave us alone in here with all this poo?? It stinks in here. It's nasty! I want OUT of here . . . NOW!!' The other little boy was the opposite. He was smiling wide engrossed by shoveling fast into the poo pile! He looked up happily and said, 'With all this poo in here . . . there's bound to be a pony SOMEWHERE!!'"

I remember this parable when I am knee-deep in it. I am at choice. I can whine and complain and blame or I can be grateful for the opportunity life has just presented to me.

I spent a good portion of my life sitting in the corner and scowling, instead of realizing how I respond to life creates my experiences.

According to R. Otto and C. G. Jung a *numinous* experience is "the psychological phenomenon of a suddenly appearing, extremely enigmatic and fascinating state in which one feels influenced by higher powers.

I think we all have numinous experiences. If you are like me; you may not remember them or trust your intuition. Yet, I had one on October 19, 2002.

I started drinking alcohol and using drugs when my best friend died in May 1966. For the next 36 years, I lived my life as a high functioning addict. There were times I stopped, and I always went back. My addiction was a slow form of suicide. Guilt and shame can be all-consuming.

I put myself in situations that were physically and emotionally dangerous to my being. One day, I had an epiphany. I instinctively knew that I would succeed in my quest for self-destruction if I did not change my behavior. Although in some circles they refer to this as *hitting bottom*, my experience was more like *waking up*.

As I opened to the idea of taking responsibility for my responses to the events in my life; my life changed. Not with lightning bolts and not in an instance, now I believe every step and every breath I took brought me to that very moment when I woke up on October 19, 2002.

I went out the night before with a friend. A usual night of drinking and drugs and yet sometime between passing out in bed and waking up the next morning, a shift happened. I woke up knowing that I was done: done drinking, done using drugs, done smoking cigarettes. To this day, I have no desire to drink or smoke or use. And I realize, my choices throughout my life brought me to that moment.

That is why it is important to be grateful. Not only for the good things in your life, not only for the people that you love, GRATITUDE is the secret ingredient to life. We all seek and forget how simple it is to say; Thank you, God.

Thank you, God; I didn't die in the birth canal. Thank you, God, I survived every abusive relationship I put myself in. Thank you, God, my boys grew up to be great fathers even though that wasn't their experience. Thank you, God . . .

So, you're probably thinking, really?? I know I was that person. I was caught up in the poor, pitiful me syndrome I wouldn't have believed anyone if they had said — just be grateful. And yet there are actual scientific studies that support the idea that people who are grateful are happier, more well-rounded individuals.

I made one BIG change around gratitude. I stopped having a gratitude practice and started being grateful ceaselessly.

Here are 7 Scientifically Proven Benefits of Gratitude that will motivate you from Amy Morin, Psychotherapist and International Bestselling Mental Strength Author and my take on them.

1. Gratitude opens the door to more relationships.

Not only more relationships, but also the right relationships. I believe each one of us is an energy center that attracts what we are putting out into the world. When I stopped feeling sorry for myself . . . SURPRISE . . . I no longer attracted people into my life who blamed everything on somebody else.

2. Gratitude improves physical health.

My right arm was constantly in pain. And I let everyone know about it. I went through this phase of thinking people should know I was hurting. Then an interesting thing happened. I stopped complaining about my arm, which pulled the focus off the pain. My arm didn't seem to hurt as much or as often.

3. Gratitude improves psychological health.

They (I'm never really sure who they are) say it is difficult to be angry or sad when you smile. I believe it and if you can't smile, be grateful. Trust me, there is always something to be grateful for. Sometimes it is remembering that today, you are above ground and breathing. One caveat here: if you suffer from depression or any type of mental illness, please seek professional help.

4. Gratitude enhances empathy and reduces aggression.

I am an impatient driver. Twenty years ago, I was an aggressive driver. I have learned the best way to counter my impatience is to practice gratitude. If someone cuts in front of me, bless them, they must really need to get where they are going. If someone is driving 20 miles an hour below the speed limit and I can't pass them, then, I need to slow down, breathe and say to myself, "There must be a reason I need to slow down."

5. Grateful people sleep better.

This has proven true in my life. I no longer lay in bed rerunning conversations that happened during the day. I call it my monkey-mind. Gratitude keeps it at bay because when I stay in gratitude, I am less argumentative and more understanding.

6. Gratitude improves self-esteem.

I am a staunch believer that you must love yourself fully before someone else can truly love you. I have learned to be grateful for the way I look, my age, my hips, you name it. People learn how to treat me based on how I treat myself.

7. Gratitude increases mental strength.

I'll admit, I am not always grateful when life hands me a bowl full of lemons. And yet, what I know for sure is that when I look back at every upset in my life, I find the revelation — also known as the pony parable!

A close friend of mine recently reminded me, I am a Gratitude Guru. When she said it, it made me laugh. I guess I am more like the fairy that sprinkles optimism and gratitude each day. Since June 2016, every morning without fail I send out a text: Rev. Gayle's Wake-up Call.

Some people respond, most don't. What I realize is that the texts are more for me, anyway.

And please, REMEMBER: E+R=O. If you want less drama in your life, live a life of gratitude. I am living proof, it works! ✷

THE BOOK ON GRATITUDE

Notes

Penny Bongato

Penny Bongato is the first Filipino to be Certified on the Success Principles and the Advanced Canfield Methodology by Jack Canfield.

She is a credentialed Associate Certified Coach (ACC) by the International Coaching Federation.

Penny is a motivational speaker, success coach trainer and author. Penny's story, Proudly Filipino, can be found in Jack Canfield's book, Living the Success Principles. She has written three books: Career Shift Follow Your Passion, (Foreword by Jack Canfield), Ask for a Bigger Blanket, Wag Mamaluktot Pag Maikli ang Kumot (Don't Curl Up when given a short blanket, ask for one), and an e-book, Forward Shift Managing Your Life at the Time of a Pandemic, Guidance from Mentors and Coaches Across the World was released in May 2020.

Penny is in no. 6 in LinkedIn's Top 100 Influential Filipino Women to Follow (2022) and also in the Top 100 Filipinos for Inspiration and Motivation in LinkedIn (2019-2021).

Contact

Website: www.pennybongato.com

Choosing Gratitude

By Penny Bongato

*"Charlie Brown: We only live once, Snoopy.
Snoopy: Wrong! We only die once. We live every day!"*

— Peanuts by Charles M. Schulz

My heart was pounding as I sat perfectly still. It was a quiet morning in the hospital. I could almost hear my own heartbeat. I stared blankly into the off-white walls of the waiting area, barely noticing that there were other people in the room. Maybe they were also waiting in limbo for news of either a miracle or a tragedy.

More than an hour had passed since *Tatang (Sammy is his name)*, my husband of 36 years, was wheeled into the operating room. I had been motionless since. Afraid to move. Thinking that the slightest foot twitch might somehow affect the outcome of his operation. Better to sit still. Still and silent.

The opposite went on in my mind. As time passed, panic flooded my thoughts. *What if the cancer metastasized? What if it spread now? What if something happens to him? What would happen to our life? I wouldn't be able to handle it . . . I just couldn't . . . I'm not ready. I will never be ready.* It was like my brain was short-circuiting. I couldn't process how my life would be without my husband, and yet

I couldn't stop thinking about the worst-case scenario.

It all happened so fast. Two days before our routine anti-pneumonia and anti-flu shots led to an impromptu checkup for *Tatang*. Subsequent tests and consultations with specialists found five cysts in different parts of his body.

My husband is one tough cookie. He already survived cancer twice, colon and prostate. But this is also why the doctors advised to remove all five cysts. They scheduled his surgery as soon as possible. When all five cysts have been removed, they would be tested for malignancy. As if waiting for the operation to be over wasn't torture enough.

Realizing that sitting motionless might cut off oxygen and blood circulation in my body, I stood up, walked around the hallway, and let my mind wander.

My brain decided to think back to a movie I had recently watched. It was entitled, "Courageous." One of the characters lost a nine-year-old daughter because of a hit-and-run by a drunk driver. There was a scene where he was talking to a pastor. "How am I supposed to let her go?" he asked. The pastor told him, "The hard choice for you is whether you're going to be angry for the time you didn't have with her or grateful for the time that you did have."

This led me to a realization. Tatang and I have been together for more than four decades. I should be grateful for my life with him. I AM grateful for my life with him. I know that it is not yet the end. But that one inevitable day will come. When it does, I don't want to be bitter. I want to be grateful.

And so, I prayed . . . *Thank you Lord for all these years of Tatang and me together. Thy will be done, but please whisper many more years with him.*

I prayed for the operation to go well. Thankfully, it did. Reunited, both of us were in tears.

After a week, we received the biopsy results. We saw the word "malignancy" in the documents, so we quickly made our way to the doctor to interpret the results. On the car ride, I was calm on the outside but distressed on the inside. I continued to pray for a benign verdict and never stopped praying since the operation or since the cysts were found.

THE BOOK ON GRATITUDE

After carefully reading the results, the doctor told us that the cysts were benign. It turned out that we read "R/O malignancy," which meant "rule out malignancy." A mixture of laughter and tears of joy and released anxiety followed.

The first words out of *Tatang* were, "Thank you, Lord!"

The next day was my birthday. That good news was the best gift I received. We celebrated with the Lord at mass in church.

When you feel like your world is falling apart, seek for courage in gratitude. When I was afraid of losing my soulmate, I drew strength from the life and time we have shared together. I knew that I will always have that no matter what happens. And I am so grateful for the many years we already shared together.

An attitude of gratitude changes everything, especially the way we think and look at life. Despite hard times, gratitude opens our eyes to the best parts of life.

Always choose to be grateful.

Ann Smith Gordon

Ann is a gifted writer and photographer whose roots go back to the Sealing of the Magna Carter in 1215 and to Richard Norwood who produced Bermuda's first survey in 1616. Ann's life of service began as a child when she carried around a nurse's bag containing all the medical equipment necessary for a five year old nurse. She graduated as a Registered Nurse in 1956.

She has served Bermuda as a tourist guide, lobster diver, business owner and President and CEO of PALS-Cancer Care in Bermuda for 33 years retiring at age 80 and continues on the Board. Ann has received numerous awards: Most prestigious as an MBE [Member of the Most Excellent Order of the British Empire] "For Services to the Community of Bermuda" by Queen Elizabeth II at Buckingham Palace in 1996.

Ann resides at her charming waterside home where her writing continues laced with wit and memories of life on the treasured Isle of Bermuda.

A Life of Gratitude

By Ann Smith Gordon, MBE, JP

"When it comes to life, the critical thing is whether you take things for granted or take them with gratitude."

— K.G. Chesterton, 1874-1936

The above quote uttered by English writer and philosopher many years ago could not be more accurate in describing my entire life. I am so thankful that I have never taken anything for granted, therefore I have seldom been disappointed.

I have so much in my life to be grateful for that I hardly know where to begin.

Let's begin at the very beginning even before my own arrival in this world in 1935 on the beloved island of Bermuda which lies alone in the great Atlantic Ocean far from any other land.

How grateful I am that my dear Scottish Mother in 1931 was visiting Cowes, the popular seaside town on the Isle of Wight in Southern England. Cowes is famous the world over for Cowes Week. It was first held in 1820 where one of the oldest and most respected sailing regattas in the world takes place every year during early August.

It was here, where my Mother met millionaire John Seward Johnson, heir to the well-known Johnson & Johnson pharmaceutical fortune. He must have been impressed with Mother as he immediately invited her to come to his home in New Brunswick, New Jersey in the United States to act as Governess to his four children, Mary Lea, Elaine, Seward and Diana. No time was lost in accepting this invitation which soon led Mother to Bermuda.

But this was not to be before her journey by steamer across the Atlantic Ocean to New York where she had the unnerving and frightening experience of being quarantined at Ellis Island, America's first federal immigration station and "thrown amongst hundreds of gangster's molls" as described by my terrified Mother. Allowed only one telephone call she was able to contact millionaire Mr. Johnson who secured her release but not before being able to prove he had enough money to employ her and that she would not become a public charge! Thus, Mother took up residence in the very comfortable New Brunswick home of the Johnson family.

This was the dawn of the 1930's and kidnapping was described as the feature crime of the time. The most famous kidnapping in the United States history took place when the twenty-month-old infant was taken from the Lindberg home not far from the Johnson estate. The father, Charles Lindberg, was famous and greatly admired for his strength and courage in his epic 1927 solo flight across the Atlantic Ocean to Paris. The discovery of his beautiful baby's body two months later caused more revulsion and grief than any other crime against a private citizen. This terrible tragedy and fear caused Mr. and Mrs. Johnson to pack up their family with Mother and the gang on the 9th of January 1933. They arrived safely on the beautiful cruise ship Monarch of Bermuda at #1 Shed in Hamilton, the capital of Bermuda with the four Johnson children and 45 pieces of luggage! For this I am eternally grateful.

The family settled into the waterside home known as Pembroke Hall built in the 1700's, owned by the Dill family whose Bermuda roots date back to the 17th century. Mrs. Johnson, a born Bermudian was Ruth Dill, and part of the prominent Bermuda family. Her sister, Diana married famous actor, Kirk Douglas, and they produced another famous actor, Michael Douglas.

Mother had barely set foot on this beautiful island before she vowed to spend the rest of her life here. Before long she met my Bermudian Dad at an afternoon tea party and they married on 31st May 1934 under one of the Royal Palm trees in the garden at Pembroke Hall. Mr. Johnson gave Mother away and all the children took part as attendants.

I was born on 20th May 1935 at 8.10 in the morning and ten days later Mother and I were discharged from the King Edward VII Memorial Hospital. In those days seven to ten days hospitalization after giving birth was considered normal. I am sure I enjoyed my first horse drawn carriage ride as we arrived at our Paget home. Actually there was no other transportation for us at the time other than a pedal bicycle!

I became another born Bermudian whose roots can be traced to before the Sealing of the Magna Carter in 1215. As I pen these words in 2022, my head is filled to the brim with so much gratitude. We have now entered the third year of the global Corona Virus pandemic and all its variants and I am surviving another quarantine. The first was in 1943 when I had to be taken to America for diagnosis and treatment for an unknown life threatening illness which turned out to be allergies to almost everything on the face of this earth. I was limited to a diet of only five foods and eventually after a year one food was added at a time. Injections were twice a week and then once a week for several years. How grateful I was to be thriving. This was an enormous emotional strain let alone a financial one on my parents. It was also the time of the highly contagious polio epidemic, a painful, terrifying and crippling disease sweeping through America during the warm summer months of 1943 and 1944. Every child was vulnerable and we were quarantined for months. How lucky brother Jamesie and I were not to be infected and managed to survive.

After two years the U.S. Department of Immigration "invited" our family to leave the United States. The terrible World War II was over at last and we were happy to be home again in Bermuda. I was eternally grateful to Dr. Hunt for making a diagnosis and saving my life. By now, I was 10 years of age and we lived in a modest home in a lovely part of Bermuda known as Fairylands. There were many families and children my age nearby and it was easy for me to make friends. I was aware of the financial hardships endured by Mother and Dad due to my illness. They both worked extremely hard to sustain our lives. It could not have been easy financially to enroll me in BHS (Bermuda High School), a private school for girls founded in 1894 based on the lines of Cheltenham Ladies College in England. When the school fees went up to 12 pounds sterling [I think the exchange rate was about $1.92] Mother and Dad were not sure I would be able to continue. How grateful I was to be able to remain but at some hardship to my parents. It was an easy bicycle ride to school and we children often met under the Royal Poinciana tree at the crossroads to ride together.

All my friends lived in bigger houses with parents who were affluent. I am grateful never to have felt resentment. By the time I was 12 or 13 most of those friends were taking group tennis lessons on Saturday mornings and in the beginning I went along and watched them from the bench. I hated to ask Mother and Dad who worked so hard if I could join them, knowing we had no extra money and besides I did not even have a tennis racquet.

One of my best friends asked her tennis-playing Dad if he had an extra racquet and he kindly gave me one. So, I joined the group for a course of ten lessons. The only formal lessons I ever had. I did not tell my parents when the ten lessons were up, so I was back on the bench again. I still went with the gang on Saturday mornings and learned a lot from the sidelines.

The coaches were very kind to me and gave me tips along the way and within a couple of years that same friend and I won the Girls Under 18 Doubles Championship and I went on to win, over the years many championships locally.

In those days various items in silver were given as prizes and I am happy to say I have a sizable collection! In the 1960's a dear and older generous millionaire tennis friend wanted to sponsor me to go on the tennis circuit. I was most appreciative, indeed flattered, but declined his generous offer as in my heart I knew I was not good enough and besides, I did not have enough of the killer instinct necessary to be successful.

Later on, in the 1980's and 1990's I ended my so-called tennis career as being assistant tennis coach for many years at the beloved Coral Beach and Tennis Club. I know that Mother and Dad were very happy and proud of me. They both always came to the tournaments when I was playing a competitive match. Mother was a nervous wreck in the stands while Dad could always be spotted watching from the nearest bush! I think they both felt the fees for those ten lessons so long ago were well spent! I am also reminded that Mother recited for many years that from about age five, while watching tennis at Coral Beach, I pronounced that someday I would be the champion on these courts! Dreams do come true!

Soon all my friends went off to boarding schools in America, Canada and England. Again thankfully, I did not resent not being able to join them as by now my heart had long been set on becoming a Registered Nurse. I had to wait until I was eighteen to enter the School of Nursing in America.

I am eternally grateful for being born on this glorious island. It is indeed a land of the sun and sea for the casual visitor but to look a little further it is also so much more. I am convinced that living anywhere else in the world for me could never have been so fulfilling. Could never have been so exciting. Could never have been so eventful.

As children we were besotted with Princess Elizabeth and Princess Margaret Rose and I dreamed hopeless dreams about being invited to Buckingham Palace. But guess what? Not only have I been presented to Her Majesty Queen Elizabeth II on four occasions, but I was invited to Buckingham Palace in 1996 to be invested by the Queen herself. She pinned the medal on my chest as a Member of the Most Excellent Order of the British Empire established in 1917 by King George V.

The ceremony took place in the magnificent Ball Room and is another wonderful story in itself. Not only that but in 1994 during a Royal Visit to Bermuda, the Governor was commanded by the Queen to invite me to her private dinner party at Government House. Another memorable event never to be forgotten.

Where else in the world would First Day Cover Stamps of the Royal Visit taken from my photographs and now in the Queen's Royal Stamp collection be possible?

There have been many other instances for which I am grateful. For example, scuba diving with the elite divers of Bermuda but missing a dive with the renowned Jacques Cousteau as I was committed to nursing a patient in the hospital at that time. I am thankful to have been President & CEO [rather lofty titles!] of a most beloved and respected cancer nursing charity for over thirty years. I traveled on stimulating and carefully researched trips to many parts of the world on annual holidays.

I have not taken the wonderful events of my life for granted. I have cherished and been grateful for so many incredible opportunities not possible for others. At the same time I do not remember questioning all the challenges, but I have always believed that one needs to make things happen rather than sitting back and hoping.

Certainly, I am and always have been grateful for small mercies as well as all the amazing experiences along the path of my life. I have been very lucky, and hope that you, too, will be able to find and celebrate the gratitude in your life. ✷

THE BOOK ON GRATITUDE

Notes

Sarah McCalden is a money and business coach, and Success Principles mentor and trainer. She helps people release their fears around money, earn the money they deserve and create their most fully expressed lives. She also works with colleges and schools to provide for their staff and students through self-esteem and success education programs that produce results.

Sarah overcame a life-threatening addiction in her 20's and got a second chance at life. This second chance has influenced her greatly in the years since and has allowed her to create a truly exciting and wonderful life.

Sarah lives in London, UK with her Kiwi husband, two sons and their cat, enjoying the best of both city life and the countryside.

Contact
Website: www.sarahmccalden.com

Helping Me Live

By Sarah McCalden

> *"We learned about gratitude and humility —
> that so many people had a hand in our success."*
>
> — Michelle Obama

I met David on New Year's Day 2003, while I was working my first shift in a night club. By that stage, I had already tried drugs again. Over the previous three months, after being clean and sober for 3 years, I had started smoking marijuana again. I had injected heroin more than once and I had tried crack cocaine.

I remember he was wearing a green striped suit and he was Scottish — like me. At the end of the night, he offered everyone a drink, but didn't have one himself. I asked for a lemonade because I didn't drink alcohol. He was surprised I didn't drink and then said he hadn't had a drink in two years next week. Well, I knew that unless you were clean and sober and a friend of Bob's, the likelihood of anyone knowing exactly when they had their last drink was slim to none.

I told David that I had tried to help a heroin addict friend get clean and sober, but my curiosity had gotten the better of me and I had tried it. I didn't think, on that day, that a full-blown heroin addiction was in my future. He told me he would take me to an AA (Alcoholics

Anonymous) meeting. I hadn't been to a meeting since I'd left the States, but I went with him the following week.

Then, another Scottish guy came up from the basement. He was a curious fellow, and it was clear he and David had known each other for a long time, but weren't exactly friends. He took my attention, immediately. He was charismatic, told me everything I wanted to hear, and I went back to his house that night. We walked through all the fancy parts of London, through Victoria, through Soho, through Bloomsbury. "Wow, I thought, how amazing and beautiful, is London?!" He took me to an old, dilapidated 2nd floor flat in the heart of Kings Cross. We sat on the floor of a grey, bare room that stank of rotten sweat, stale cigarettes and burnt metal. He pulled out an empty plastic coke bottle, made a hole in it for a pipe and smoked crack right in front of me. He asked me if I wanted some. I said no. But it was only a couple more nights like this, before I said yes, and crack cocaine had its full power over me. It was some months later, that I started using heroin on a regular basis.

At some point that February, I recognized that I had become a shell of my previous self. I had lost an incredible amount of weight and all I could think about was smoking crack. My goals and dreams focused around getting more drugs and it was difficult to think an hour ahead, never mind a day or a week. For the next five years, I lived there in Kings Cross, addicted to crack cocaine and heroin, always wanting more. It was my only priority. My only goal was to get money to get high.

There was a part of me that knew I needed help early on, so I continued to meet David every now and again and go to a Cocaine Anonymous meeting, but it was fleeting. I didn't really have an interest in getting clean, most of the time. I had become ill. I was really ill, and I got worse.

The next five years were the worst of my life in many respects. I was helpless, hopeless and resigned, most of the time to the fact that I would die using drugs. I couldn't see any way out of that life. There was no other way out, except death. At times, I'd made a conscious effort to go to Cocaine Anonymous and Alcoholics Anonymous, and I would get a day clean, or few days clean, or a few weeks clean, and even on an occasion or two, a few months clean. And then I would relapse, destroying all trust and any belief in myself, that I could stop; that I could end that nightmare of a life. I didn't believe anyone cared about me, at all, and I felt useless, unlovable, and incredibly unworthy.

But there was always someone there, on the other end of the phone, when I called David. He always had time to help me. And he probably had time like this, for countless others. David had his own issues. He was also a recovering alcoholic and addict, but one thing I knew for sure, was that he found — and still finds — meaning in helping others. He would talk to me for hours on the phone. He would meet me and take me to meetings after I'd relapse. Even when I couldn't face anyone because I felt so awful and small and worthless, he would help me to get to a meeting.

There are many things I am grateful for. Practicing gratitude is a daily occurrence for me, but there are some people in my life, who will always have my heart and my gratitude, forever, because they helped me live.

I met Craig on a Saturday evening in December 2004. I was so sick and ashamed of myself, I could no longer face going to Cocaine Anonymous because I felt worse than humiliated, I felt wholly inadequate, showing up, relapse after relapse. I thought I would try a Narcotics Anonymous meeting, about 5 minutes' walk from where I lived in Kings Cross. It was the only NA meeting I ever went to in London. I couldn't speak at that meeting, for my anxiety was so strong. Even saying "I'm Sarah, I'm an addict" seemed so tortuously difficult. After the meeting, one of the guys who had been there went outside and pulled out a cigarette, so I asked him for one. I didn't have any and the corner shop near home wouldn't give me anymore without paying. I took the cigarette and asked him for a lighter and walked back to the flat.

I called David on my way home. He asked me why I was going back home. I didn't really know.

There was a meeting in Chelsea, on the other side of central London, that Sunday afternoon so I headed there. I was in the mood to get clean. I noticed the guy from the NA meeting, the night before. He showed up and when it was his turn, he said, "Hi I'm Craig, and I'm an addict." He had an Australian accent. I left that meeting and didn't go back for about a month. Of course, that was because I was relapsing. The next time I headed to that Sunday afternoon meeting, Craig was collecting his 30-Day Chip. When I saw him get up and get it, I felt so angry and ashamed of myself. WHY — WHHHHHHHHYYYYYYY could I not just stay clean and sober?! I thought to myself, "I would have 30 days behind me, if I had done what he did." I decided I would try again. I thought, if this guy can do it, so can I. My new clean date was the 8th January 2005. I lasted for less than a week and went back on the gear. But I had found a friend in Craig even when I didn't want him to be a friend, and as a result of his friendship, I did manage to get a lengthy period of several months clean during the next little while.

Craig was always, always, always there for me. We would meet at CA meetings often. I remember he would take me to the cinema, buy me food and take me out to dinner when I was starving, buy me coffees and share his cigarettes with me, and he even bought me an iPod, so I could listen to music. I cherished that thing but battled deeply with my feelings of unworthiness. I felt so undeserving of it. That little iPod was such a special gift to me at the time. He knew music would help me, and it did. He believed in me, when I felt like I was nothing, when I was a shell of a person, when I felt like dying. He was there for me. Until he moved to Hong Kong.

Later in 2006, I decided really, there was no return to Cocaine Anonymous for me. I was too full of shame, for the last time, I told myself. I went to an AA meeting near Portland Street, near Regent's Park. I met a woman that day, called Katherine. She sounded American. It had been about five years since I had lived in the States at that time. I really liked her. I got on with her, properly. I could talk to her about things, I just hadn't been able to talk about for years. It's like, I had been a mute, repressed, suppressed, oppressed, even, and knowing her, allowed me to build more of "me" back into that shell I had become. I met up with Katherine almost daily after our AA meetings and we had so much fun together. We were cunning and sly and tricky, and we enjoyed it! And I stayed sober as a result.

At different points in my journey, David, Craig and Katherine were the true heroes in my life. They are the people I am most grateful to and for, even all these years later. They helped me through really, the toughest times of my life, with their caring, gentle, fun-loving, kind and generous natures. I was not certain I was going to live through it. I am grateful to David for always being on the end of the phone, for keeping me entertained and for meeting me anywhere, practically anytime and taking me to a meeting, when I needed it the most. I am grateful to Craig, for being such a great friend to me. For seeing the things in me, that I couldn't see, and for giving me so much love, that I didn't fully appreciate at the time. Katherine and I were proper friends for about eight months. Without Katherine's friendship, I'm not sure where I would be right now. These people did not do the hard yards for me, they did that for themselves. They made my life a little more joyful, a little more fun, a little more exciting, enough to hang onto hope, and to keep on living, and for that, I am grateful.

I have lived such a great life since getting clean and sober.

It certainly didn't happen overnight, but in recovering, I learned to practice gratitude every day, morning and night and throughout the day.

Now, my gratitude practice looks very different to when I started many years ago, but still, there is not a day that goes by, where I do not have gratitude for these three very important people. They affected my life in such positive and profound ways. They were there at the beginning and they helped me live — THEY HELPED ME LIVE — and go on to accomplish so much.

What they did for me, knowingly or unknowingly was profound, and I am forever grateful to each of them. Their gifts of support and love fuel my desire to help others feel the gratitude that I do in every minute of every beautiful day.

Jane Williams

Jane Williams is an Intuitive Energy Coach & Performing Arts Educator who helps people break through blocks to become the most abundant and best version of themselves. As a graduate of Michigan State University, Virginia Tech and The Dell'Arte School of Physical Theatre, Jane has worked in the performing arts and creativity field all her life. Jane is a Dow Creativity Fellow from Northwood University in Michigan and an Emerging Artist Recipient from the Durham Arts Council in North Carolina.

She has completed Jack Canfield's & Kathleen Seeley's Success Principles Virtual Skills Bootcamp; is on her RIM journey with Dr. Deb Sandella; and is a Certified Barrett Values Centre Leadership & Coaching Consultant. Often referred to as "The Intuitive Archeologist," Jane continually looks for the best in people and how to unravel the "puzzle" of who they are and wish to become. She has deep gratitude for being included here with Jan and her co-authors!

Contact
Website: www.janeawilliams.com
Email: jane@janeawilliams.com

The Gratitude of Connection

By Jane Williams

""Today's gratitude is for unexpected connections, last minute trips, the potential, the actual, the seeing about things, saying yes, let's just see what happens, yes."

— Silvi, TheMindsJournal.com

People are leaving right now. Vacating place and planet. Transitioning. Journeying on. While I am thankful, or should I say *grateful*, for still remaining, it becomes tough when it all hits at once. Losses that leave gapes in my soul and life. Rendered holes that are filled with great ennui and are challenging to describe to others. People and places in my beingness that have always been there without my realizing how much they are a fiber of me until they are quite suddenly . . . gone.

It was during one such recent loss where I was feeling my feels and not knowing what to do for a family, that I became completely bereft. My first instinct was to reach out to try and "help in any way I could;" to "help fix things and make them better." But then you know, it becomes about my grieving and not theirs. I was at a loss at what to do or say or even to whom I should do or say to. I only knew that I did not want to intrude on their very deep grief during their time of coming to grip with a very sudden loss. But, my heart was in mourning. Probably because this community had just suffered another loss and additionally, the losses in my own life felt like they kept piling up. Then out of the blue, a mutual friend reached out to make sure that I knew of this loss. "Hey, — Ane (one of many nicknames given to me over the years), I hope all is well with you. Did you hear about . . ." And yes. Yes I had. As we continued to chat through messenger, my heart felt lighter and I felt much more connected to myself and this grieving community. Where there had been shadow, there was now lightness and buoyancy. I can only hope he felt as I did — needing to talk but not knowing where to turn — but maybe he didn't. All I know is, that by his reaching out to inform me, I was able to create a much-needed connection through time and space, placing me in a time of laughter and fond memories with each other and a community we both knew who were also in mourning.

I realized later that I felt deep gratitude for this random connection. My friend could not know what I was feeling at the time but through his thoughtfulness of checking in with me to inform of this incident, he rested my heart for a moment in time. He didn't know just how much the time meant to me where we first met and got to know each other, nor that I have carried it in my heart and memories since then. He does now though and this one random connection over messenger, lifted my heart so very much.

I have GRATITUDE for this connection. And I always will.

Last fall I was involved in an automobile accident in my home state of Michigan. This happened in the very early hours of the morning as I was trying to catch a flight home to my current state of residence of North Carolina. Two vehicles totaled; every single one of my air bags exploded; glass everywhere; and I was sent to the hospital for scans and x-rays. Needless to say, I missed all my flights, was now without a car, and . . . I felt very scared and very alone.

Thankfully, I quickly learned I wasn't alone. I had people who cared enough to drive two and a half hours one way to pick me up from one city and drive me two and a half hours (through much ribbing because

I was now not only a saxophonist, but carless and homeless as well) back home to their own city. This was so I could stay with another dear friend to convalesce and be watched over. They wanted to make sure I didn't fall and crack my head open NOR get on a plane *that very second* as I was bound and determined to do . . . as I apparently kept repeating to anyone who would listen. "No, Yane (another nickname), you have to stay put!" So stayed put I did until I felt well enough to re-book my flights and travel later in the week. All during this time I was able to check with touchstones, again on messenger, that helped me to think things through one step at a time until everyone helped me figure things out. Much later, I realized that yes, I could have stayed in a hotel but by informing others of my plight, the matter was quickly taken out of my hands and a much better environment was provided for me.

I am so grateful to belong to an elite group of friends and musicians who really care about each other. The Spartan Marching Band and my fellow music majors from Michigan State University are the BEST people in the world and are truly my family. And, as more folks learned of what had happened to me, the offers of help poured in from even more of my true family of people I had grown up with and are blessed to know.

Yes, this incident was not the best thing to ever happen to me. And yet, somehow, it was. I have deep gratitude for all these amazing friends in my life who drop things to help a homeless and carless saxophonist. I have so much deep and humble gratitude for the comfort and care of friends I hadn't even met yet through the many random folks who stopped to help — fellow travelers, paramedics, police and fire officers, medical personnel — even my doctor and nurse running my scans and x-rays at the hospital were, as it turned out, fellow musicians. All of these people took such good care of me throughout this whole process and for months afterwards.

I have GRATITUDE for these connections. And I always will.

One day while at home, I was sitting in my comfy chair lost in thought of, well, really nothing. The glass doors to my deck were open and I was enjoying a balmy breeze coming in through the screen doors. My flowers were bright and bountiful. As I watched the bumblebees work my flowers, they were so heavy with pollen that they could barely fly as flecks dropped off their legs. And yet, they kept coming back for more and more of their sought-out gold. With the lazy droning of their wings, the bumbles, as plentiful as they found the pollen to be, helped me to relax further into the nothingness of my daydreams. The breeze made everything shimmer and sway as Louie, on duty at the screen doors as my resident guard cat, hunkered down and watched for anything that dare move onto his turf. Secretly, I knew he was enjoying that beautiful breeze just as much as I was, but I just let him stand guard in order to keep the peace. Voices from neighbors, the barks of dogs and the chirps of birds floated on the air in the background. It was that kind of day. All was calm. All was content. A nothing day that wasn't anything special except for anchoring me; connecting me in the moment and this world of ours.

I have GRATITUDE for this connection. And I always will.

The commonality found here for me from each of these very different moments of my life is one of connection. Of reaching out through thoughtfulness of information to me in the first moment. Of basically coming to save me in so many ways in the second moment. Of nature grounding me in the third moment. Connection between myself to other people and to the world, all while lifting my heart and placing me in times of laughter and fond memories. The moments of bringing light into a weary heart and soul from a single person, a group of people, or even from bumblebees coated in pollen. Light that comes blazing into the moments of despair, grief, fear and loneliness to illuminate that I am never truly alone. I have deep gratitude for every moment of my life that transcends me to another place and time and into a much better person as each of these moments have. I feel so grateful and fortunate to be honored by so many light-bearers in my life. Because of these amazing people and wondrous moments in my life, I have learned — albeit slowly and densely — to reach out when the shadows start creeping in. Because where there are at least two, there is light. And because of my love and wonderment of nature, I have learned that sometimes all I need to do is just pause and pull the light in only by breathing in the nothingness of the day.

I recently had a friend tell me that, "We have AMAZING lives, Yanie! Look at the people we know and have in our lives! Feel glad instead of sad!" I think this very good friend of mine, was not only telling me to "buckle-up buttercup," but was also telling me to take heart and LIVE in these moments of connection.

For these are the moments that create such deep, deep gratitude. Grief, fear, despair and loneliness not only take great love, passion and courage with which to feel and live them, but also a willingness to engage with those people and our surroundings.

I know that I am truly fortunate to have so many really good folks in my life. I know that it is a blessing to be able to feel deeply. I know that I am delighted to continue to receive such wonderment in the simple things of nature.

I have GRATITUDE for these connections.

And I always will.

JAN FRASER INSPIRED LIFE SERIES

Choosing GRATITUDE

Sina Ciampa

Sina is a passionate elementary school teacher, loving wife of 25 years to Bruno and mom to her 2 amazing teenage daughters Emily and Melissa in Ontario, Canada.

Her passions include traveling, playing volleyball, hot yoga, preparing healthy recipes and learning about the Law of Attraction. If you're lucky, you might catch her singing and dancing to 80s music!

Sina is genuinely grateful for all of the blessings she has received and continues to receive. She teaches gratitude to her students and encourages them to look for all the good things in life.

Contact
Email: qootee29@gmail.com

For This, I am Grateful

By Sina Ciampa

"At times our own light goes out and is rekindled by a spark from another person. Each of us has cause to think with deep gratitude of those who have lighted the flame within us."

— Albert Schweitzer

It's not easy being the first-born child to a first-generation Italian immigrant family. There were no celebrations, no birthday parties, Christmas gifts or vacations. As a young child, I compared myself to my classmates. I just thought we were poor. As my friends talked about what they did on the weekend with their parents, I became jealous. Not of the trips or the gifts. The one thing I wanted the most, was love.

My dad worked all the time as a water maintenance worker for the City of Toronto. Because of this, he always had a bad temper. He would take his anger out on everybody. I learned to 'read him' as he arrived home from work and when it looked like the calm before the storm, I would retreat to my bedroom. He was not an affectionate man towards me. In fact, I never saw him smile. I feared even being in the same room with him. If my father couldn't love me, then who would?

My mother had a part time job as a PSW (Personal Support Worker) and always made sure there was a meal waiting for us. She did her best trying to give me and my brother a normal life by taking us to church every Sunday followed by the occasional trips to Mcdonald's. My parents seemed to co-exist. I never saw any love or even kind words between the two of them. What I did see was constant heated arguments with the fear that my mom would be hurt by my dad. I'm certain that all those years of arguing is what eventually led to her diagnosis of Alzheimer's at the age of 72.

But this is not a story about a sad childhood. It's a love story. My first love was teaching. I knew I always wanted to teach. As a small child, I would play school. I would line up all my stuffed toys on my bed and read them a story or give them spelling tests. I must have been a great teacher because they always got perfect scores. As I always attended church on Sundays, naturally when the time came that they needed volunteers to run the children's liturgy, I did. Children's liturgy is when we gather all the children aged 5-10 to meet with volunteers in the chapel and we go over the days readings in a child friendly way. My colleague decided that this group should also start a Youth group. This sounded like fun to me because I rarely set foot outside my house unless it was school or church. In high school, I watched as all my girlfriends started dating. I was still searching, thus the idea of a youth group meeting a couple of times a month to have fun excited me. We planned movie nights, softball leagues and bowling.

On the first night, we met in the downstairs hall of the church and we were milling around getting to know each other. Suddenly, the door opens and in walked three fellows in leather jackets. WOW! They were handsome! The feeling in the room shifted. I thought they were probably in the wrong place. They affirmed that they were attending the Youth group. As the group spent more time together, I realized there was one fellow in particular who caught my eye. SPARK! His name was Bruno.

It turned out that he was interested in me, too. He asked me out on a date and we chatted over some cheesecake and coffee. I could feel the butterflies fluttering inside of me because I really liked him. Our conversation felt easy and I realized that we had similar views and values. For the first time, I felt seen and worthy of someone's attention. I brought him home to meet my mother and brother. I was nervous, wondering how this meeting would go. My mother cracked some jokes about me, but all was ok. When I met his parents, I immediately felt at home. My now mother-in-law would always load up my dinner plate with her delicious food. No wonder the first year I met his family I gained about 10+ pounds! My father-in-law was always telling a story or joking about something. He still does to this day. He is a kind, loving and generous man. I could see where Bruno got his kindness from. I was so grateful that our meetings with the parents went well.

Bruno and I dated for five years. He opened my eyes to the vastness of what was possible. There were no limits to what we did together: fishing, skiing, hiking, vacationing, dining and dancing. What intrigued me the most about our relationship was how aligned we were. We would finish each other's sentence or say what the other was thinking. When the topic of marriage came up, I told Bruno that my definition of marriage meant forever. That he shouldn't marry me if he was not ok with my own family situation. I was giving him a 'get outta jail free' card. What he said next shocked me. He said that he was marrying me, not my family.

On June 14, 1997, I said 'I do' to my soul mate. I was grateful.

Within three years of wedded bliss, tragedy hit. My beautiful daughter, Christina, was born June 27, 2000. She was angelic is every way. Her big brown eyes stared back at me and all I wanted to do was hold her. Her round and rosy cheeks summoned me to kiss her constantly. But I noticed that something was wrong when she was a month old. After nursing her, she would vomit her milk and she was always so lethargic. I took her to my family doctor who said I was an anxious first-time mom. I took my little girl home and the vomiting continued. We took Christina to numerous doctors, pediatricians and finally Sick Kid's.

We were hit with devastating news! Christina was born with a rare metabolic disorder. There wasn't much they could do. My heart split open. I questioned my faith. Why had God done this to us? We could be amazing parents to her! I spent two months living at the hospital with her. It was hard seeing her hooked up to a respirator and a feeding tube. I couldn't even pick her up. All I could do was slip in next to her in her bed and lie next to her, kissing her as often as I could.

On October 29th of the same year Christina was moved to the palliative care wing of the hospital. Christina was having a hard time breathing even with a respirator. Bruno and I crawled into her bed, one on either side of her and cocooned her. I must have dozed off, only to be awakened by Bruno saying to Christina, "It's ok," as he stroked her little cheek and she faded away.

I have never known pain as I did that day. Someone ripped my heart right out of my chest. I was an empty shell. The eyes that once gazed upon her lovingly and with great anticipation, now were clouded. I would never watch her grow up to be a beautiful woman. The days, weeks and months that followed were a blur. I didn't feel alive. What was the point of living with this pain that would not ease? Bruno never left me alone. I would burst out in tears and he remained strong for me, comforting me all the time.

This was true love. I learned to treasure my husband even more. I was grateful.

In 2002 and 2006 we welcomed our two daughters, Emily and Melissa. I didn't think I could love Bruno more than watching him be a father to our girls. To this day, he loves them with his whole heart, rough housing with them any chance he gets. When I had concerns with our daughters, he was there, with his words of reason. When I doubted my abilities as a mother, he was there, as my cheerleader. When I would come home from a bad day at work, he was there, my supporter and thoughtful ear. When I would reach my wits end with overload, there he was, booking a weekend getaway for the two of us. I was grateful.

As I write this, I am tearing up. How did I get so lucky? Some people search a lifetime for their right match.

The following quote by Tracy Hagler captures how I feel.

"My husband has made me laugh, Wiped my tears, hugged me tight, watched me succeed, seen me fail and kept me strong. As we have walked through the many seasons of life together, I'm truly thankful for the gift of marriage."

THE BOOK ON GRATITUDE

We recently celebrated our 25th anniversary. I look back at all of those years and am amazed at our journey. We had our share of highs and lows. I am grateful that we grew as individuals and as a couple. Before Bruno, I was afraid of so many things. With Bruno I feel free to explore and grow because I know he loves me unconditionally. He never judges me and I can always be myself. I learned the importance to reaching out to others in their time of need. I may not have all the answers, but I can definitely be a listening ear or quiet companion.

For my daughters, I want them to know that true love is possible and it is important to be your true authentic self. That sometimes the person you are searching for finds you when you least expect it. That a marriage with a strong foundation can weather any storm, even a death.

That you can be a part of your happily ever after. For all of this, I am truly grateful. ✤

Regina Andler

Regina Andler is a Business Mindset Transformation Specialist who helps women entrepreneurs move from overwhelmed to overjoyed in their business, guaranteed, using her proprietary From Chaos to Clients program.

She is a Jack Canfield Success Principles Certified Trainer and also certified in Wholebeing Positive Psychology.

Her passion is to help women business owners design and create the lifestyle business of their dreams by teaching them how to shift their mindset for success.

In her spare time, Regina volunteers with local non-profit organizations and she is an avid obstacle course racer.

Contact
Website: www.autumnascentconsulting.com
Email: regina@autumnascent.com

Journaling is Overrated

By Regina Andler

"Gratitude turns negative energy into positive energy. There is no situation or circumstance so small or large that it is not susceptible to gratitude's power."

— Melody Beattie

Course after course, seminar after seminar, you hear the words 'You need to start a gratitude journal.' And the sound of those words causes you to cringe.

Okay, maybe not you. Some people love to journal. I personally know people who have been faithfully journaling every single day for over ten years.

I get it. I understand the power of the written word and yet when I think about journaling, I literally feel nauseous!

For the longest time I thought to myself, 'What is wrong with me?' I really thought there was something wrong with me for my dislike of journaling. I mean all of the seminars and courses I attended swore by the power of journaling. They couldn't all be wrong, right? So, I kept trying to do it . . . and kept trying to like it.

Mentor after mentor talked about all the pros of journaling, including the fact that it raises your energy, and how, on your not-so-good days, you can go back and reread what you have been grateful for in the past to get you back into a better frame of mind. There were a lot of pros for journaling.

Why didn't I want to do it?

I spent years seeking answers as to why the idea of writing down three things I was grateful for every day did not sit well with me. After all, I express my gratitude daily, always feel grateful, so what was the deal with not wanting to write all that down in a journal? After all, it's all good!

I spent years starting and stopping journals, determined to force myself to get used to this practice.

I would go out and purchase the prettiest journals I could find thinking maybe that would help me get in the mood to journal. It didn't. I have a bookcase shelf dedicated to really pretty blank and partially filled journals.

I thought, maybe there was some limiting belief behind my dislike of journals. As a coach myself, I work with people and their limiting beliefs all the time in my business, and I will tell you, you cannot fix yourself. There is a saying in our business — 'Every coach needs a coach.'

You may think you know what your limiting beliefs are, and yet your brain is wired to protect you, quite literally, and will block the really important facts that you need to get to the bottom of your limiting beliefs. You need someone else who can see and hear what you are saying and more importantly not saying to get you to the core of your limiting belief in order to remove it.

I went out seeking assistance from multiple friends who are also skilled in helping people get to the bottom of their limiting beliefs. With each one we searched, and prodded and dug deep, looking for an answer.

In my past I had written in journals. Not about gratitude, but rather to get 'stuff' out of my head. None of it was good stuff. As a matter of fact, it was so bad, that when I finally was ready to let go of everything that I had on all those pages that spanned multiple journals, I had a little personal shredding party with just me, the journals, a shredder, and a bottle of Merlot. It was a very cathartic experience.

My 'coach' friends and I explored that idea that my brain associated journaling with writing about negative stuff and maybe that was at the root of my journaling dislike. Maybe I associated journals with bad — not good. As it turned out, that wasn't it.

I just don't like to journal. There was, however, a limiting belief.

The limiting belief we identified was that I actually believed that I had to write daily in a gratitude journal in order for me to express my gratitude and raise my vibration. If I didn't do this journaling thing, in the traditional way that all my mentors were talking about, then there was something wrong with me and I was not really expressing my gratitude properly. I had this feeling of disappointment in myself for not being able to like journaling the way everyone else did and it was holding me back.

I have to admit that I don't do much in the traditional sense. For example, I don't sit quiet and meditate. I prefer active meditation. I get my best thoughts and get most in-tune with myself when I am out walking in nature or exercising. I learned that fun fact about myself years ago and I have been an active meditator ever sense.

What made me think that sitting quietly, thoughtfully, writing in a journal about gratitude was going to work for me? Turns out that was a limiting belief that was not true for me and yet I was holding onto it as it was reinforced every time I went to another seminar or heard another mentor talk about the joys of journaling.

In the path of my own discovery, I realized that there are a lot of us who think there is something wrong with us because we cannot do these processes in the traditional way.

Turns out, we just like to do things a bit differently.

I finally accepted that there was nothing wrong with me at all. It's just that no one ever taught me that there were other ways to do it.

As a coach who is skilled in the workings of energy and vibration and teaches the power of gratitude all the time, I needed to find an outlet for my gratitude. Something that did not include writing daily in a journal.

A little side note about gratitude and energy . . .

Everything is energy. Everything, everywhere, is constantly in a state of vibration and everything vibrates at a specific frequency.

Like energy attracts like energy. That is the sole premise behind the Law of Attraction. You attract to you what you are energetically putting out there.

Gratitude is one of the highest forms of energy and on the same vibrational frequency as love and joy.

When you express gratitude every day, you are consciously setting your frequency to attract more things to be grateful for. This is why living in a state of gratitude is so amazing.

Finding gratitude in everything keeps you vibrating at a high frequency and all the bad stuff just falls away from you because it literally cannot exist at that frequency.

This is why so many coaches, teachers, and spiritual healers insist on keeping a daily gratitude journal.

With the journaling practice, when you wake up in the morning or go to bed at night and write down what you are grateful for, you are manually setting your energy dial at that high frequency and vibration.

For me, I would write faithfully for a couple weeks. Then I would miss a day writing here and there. Then it would be a week. Then the journal would end up, unfinished, on the shelf.

The fact that I would miss a day, or a week was really messing with my energy. It was like jumping up and down on an energy trampoline. When I wrote, I was up, when I missed a day, I was down, and it became a vicious cycle. I needed to find a solution that worked for me.

If you love to write in your journal, one of the great things about the action of handwriting your gratitude is that when you hand write your brain is fully engaged. Conversely, when you type on a computer, you are only using half of your brain — the logical side. When you hand write something on paper, you are using both sides of your brain, the logical and the creative. Energetically speaking, handwriting is more powerful.

Knowing this, I really wanted to get to the bottom of my journaling dilemma.

What I discovered was that journaling was like meditation for me. And if I could not sit still to meditate, why in the world would I believe I could sit still and write in a journal.

I needed to approach my gratitude practice just like meditation. I needed some form of "active journaling." I needed to engage both sides of my brain without handwriting in a book.

In my search to find another way, I came across a powerful tool to help me harness the power of my gratitude without writing one word in a journal.

As my Universe turns, I attracted to me a mentor who used a completely different way of practicing gratitude that extended far beyond just the gratitude piece.

I was introduced to what she called her daily practice of "GID" — "Gratitude, Intentions, and Delegations."

As she explained to me, every day, at the beginning of the day, she states out loud what she is grateful for, followed by her intentions for the day and then her delegations.

It may go something like this, "I am grateful for the time I had with my family last night. I am grateful for new connections I met at yesterday's networking event. Today I intend to be focused and productive in my work and spend quality time with my family tonight. I delegate to the Universe that my day flows easily and effortlessly and that I am open and receptive to seeing everything I need to complete my tasks."

This GID practice is amazingly powerful. I personally believe it is more powerful than writing down what I am grateful for in a journal because of the addition of the intentions and delegations.

I started to incorporate this into my daily practices.

Each morning, before setting one foot out of bed, I lie there and state out loud my gratitude, intentions, and delegations for the day.

It is easy, effortless, and best of all, it feels good!

The very first day I felt my energy raise before I even set one foot out of my bed.

Using this practice daily created an amazing transformation in my energy. I found that anytime during the day, if things started to feel a bit off, I could think back on my GID for the day and remember what I was grateful for and what my intentions were for that day and raise my energy back up so I could get on with my day.

GID — stating my gratitude, intentions, and delegations — created a complete shift in the energy I was emitting. Remember, energy attracts like energy, and I began to attract more and more of what I wanted into my life, more things to be grateful for, and I continue to do so each and every day.

Do you love to journal? If so, go for it. Keeping a physical gratitude journal in which, you write every single day will keep you in a constant state of gratitude and keep your energy high.

For me, what I learned throughout my personal journey was that if I missed a day of journaling, I could actually feel the drop in my energy and that would affect me throughout my entire day.

When I stopped journaling and started my daily GID practice, it was easy and effortless to stop for a moment or two before I got out of bed in the morning and raise my energy level for the day and keep it high all day.

If you have ever had that feeling of disappointment in yourself for missing a day in your journal, then maybe it is time to try the Gratitude, Intentions and Delegations process each morning and see if that is the shift that you need in your life to raise your energy and allow you to attract more of what you want in your life.

This practice has worked wonders for me, and I am sure it can for you as well.

THE BOOK ON GRATITUDE

Notes

Beatriz Maria Centeno

Beatriz Maria is Head of PR and Global Corporate Communications for a Blog talk Radio production company, interviews hundreds of high-profile business leaders, the author for EP Magazine, writes Press Releases and scripts for the hosts Doug Llewelyn of the TV show People's Court and Jim Masters of PBS Television.

An outspoken animal rights activist, she has campaigned alongside well-known public officials who advocate for no kill animal shelters.

She is graduate of C.W. Post Long Island University with a Bachelor of Arts in English and Journalism, who spent the early part of her career working in fashion for several prestigious companies, then for a Book Club company overseeing their sales division.

A fitness enthusiast, fashionista, she also enjoys creating healthy plant-based meals, and loves banana boating and jet skiing in the Cayman Islands.

She has written several soon to be published novels/screenplays and lives with several rescue fur babies.

Contact
Email: beatrice@closeuptelevision.com

Gratitude for Compassion

By Beatriz Maria Centeno

"Gratitude begins in our hearts and seeks expression in acts of kindness."

— GratitideHabitat.com

There is a saying by John Bunyan, "You have not lived today until you have done something for someone who can never repay you." That's why I'm starting off by declaring how thankful I am for so many things. But, I could never cover them all in a short chapter in a collaborative book on gratitude. I feel privileged for this opportunity to also write about my overwhelming appreciation for the substantially growing number of people around the world increasingly concerned about protecting our most vulnerable animals.

Just the other night, I dreamt of one of my fur babies running toward me jubilantly among lush fields, her silky fur flying. And I wept. Only this time it was tears of gratitude for being fortunate to have had her in my life. My fur kids shared all my pains, struggles, triumphs, and celebrations. Because the greatest love is unconditional love, especially when you rescue these loves from the streets. They heal my heart with meows, barks, head butting, and cuddles. For anyone privileged enough to own a pet, you know precisely what I mean. Fellow animal lovers are all too familiar with one of the most gut-wrenching poems ever written, *The Rainbow Bridge*. (Anonymous Author). When I read pet tributes on the Rainbow Bridge support community website of pet parents in paralyzing grief over their beloved four-legged babies, wow, there is still true love even in these turbulent times.

I echo the quote "In my darkest hour, I reached for a hand and found a paw." From my earliest days, I had a kinship with animals and a childhood free from grown-up anxieties with hard working, self-sacrificing parents who afforded me many luxuries. I even got to attend a prestigious Catholic school in my plaid uniform skirt, shiny Mary Jane shoes, and ribbons in my hair, and overindulging in many family trips. But one especially dark day occurred when I was biking at the age of five, along with my twin sister and the seven-year-old blonde-haired boy from our neighborhood. When my sister flew off her bike and was frantically rushed to the hospital. Doctors grimly pronounced there was no hope for her survival. Through the anguished cries of my mother one doctor stepped up to perform emergency surgery, and she pulled through! Thank you, angel doctor, for giving us our miracle!

Gratitude speaks in everything I hold dear. I have photos that are nice to look at every day. One reads, "My therapist has fur and four paws", and another one: "Happiest girls are prettiest." I love waking up to the aroma of fresh brewed coffee from my little pink coffee pot and my pets making me laugh. I love to laugh. They do zoomies and chase each other, and my heart overfloods with relief that I can provide a safe and secure home for them. Outside my window, birds and squirrels nibble on sunflower seeds put out by me and my neighbors. I am so grateful for smells and colors. My intensely visual Thomas Kinkade paintings of quaint, antiquated, whimsical sugar and spice cottages remind me of old -fashioned days. My photos in elegant Ralph Lauren frames seamlessly meld past and present, of characters both haunting and memorable, not currently in my life but uniquely engraved in my memories, connected to me through life lessons.

Around the age of 10, I ventured into writing novels and poems to unleash my conflicting emotions of self-expression. Although I became world-weary, the reality of that was somewhat blurred, because my adolescent years were actually reckless; those times of being young and daring in those defiant coming-of-age years. It was both inscrutable and unfathomable, wayward and guileless. From rad vacations in idyllic islands, parties because I adored music and dancing, and being a fashion diva, to welcoming the challenges of academia, and excelling in my studies. My life was a crowning achievement of subtleties and remnants mirroring Sex in the City, Dawson Creek, and Friends. Those times were epic.

Reflecting now through grownup eyes at the girl I once was, life would have been unbearably oppressive without my close-knit family members, siblings, cousins, and friends. Then there was my soul mate, my exquisite love, the yin to my yang, even if it didn't lead to the happily ever after I imagined. Seemingly endings lead to hopelessness shrouded in futility, like smoldering ashes, forgotten and meaningless, but infinitely etched in our hearts. That's because the beautiful truth is all ex-flames are fragments of a prodigious love story. But that soul mate, that innocent, unforgettable love, is immutable, beautiful but hideous, disparaging yet hopeful, heartwarming yet melancholy, gone but eternal. I recall a time nine months into our relationship when I had planned an overseas trip with my friends. He was sullen, I was excited. Months before, he had gifted me a bracelet and to his disappointment, I hardly wore it. Preparing for my trip, I overheard sorrowful music that struck a chord in my heart and jolted me to my truth, this was my true love. In the car on the way to the airport, he solemnly reached for my hand seeking reassurance and spotted the bracelet on my wrist. A handsome smile of relief, a tender hug, an enduring moment in time.

A few years later after our forced goodbyes (because our circumstances did not allow us to be together), I moved to a new place with my loyal, never-left-my-side, four-legged babies. As I unpacked, I saw the large dusty box containing a new French Vanity desk that he had bought me months ago and I hadn't taken it out of the box yet. Being completely unhandy, I had no plans to ever assemble it myself. The old me would wait around for him to do it. The new reinvented me pulled it out of the box. And ta da, I did it! Ok . . . it took over an hour and I sweated profusely and one of the legs to this day is still wobbly, but it set the precedence for the future. Reminding me of one of my favorite movies Nadia Comaneci who proclaimed to her gymnastics coach, "Now I understand, I can do it on my own!" Then with fiery passion, she got on the balance beam and brought the team to victory.

I, too, will bring my life to victory!

Seldom could this have occurred if I only acquainted joy in my own endeavors, rather they were, amplified, through my friends and family's weddings, graduations, baptisms, milestones, and with each celebration we all planted the seeds of gratitude.

I met one of my dearest girlfriends in college and, once we became besties, I knew the world would become indecipherable without her in my life. So, when she married, and moved to another continent we never lost touch. Over the years, oceans apart, I remained guided by her bad-ass strength and independence, and she by my whimsy and candor. However, for this ravishing girl, young love turned to divorce, and she ended up moving back to the states (Florida and me in NY). Even now on somewhat jarring paths, twinkled with a smudge of obscurity, disjointed if you will, she's actually absolutely beaming, unhindered, ready for new adventures. And declaring it won't be the same if I'm not a part of it. Even in our lost dreams, a world of love and hate, despite it all, our innermost radiance sparkles, it's like we are going back in time, but of course we cannot. We are reimagining the future, in moments of contemplation, now completely uninhibited that truly transcend a life we never imagined, to the possibilities of wonderful new things. It's wonderful how friends can light up each other's path in the most unexpected ways.

At the gist of it all, remains my compassion for all living creatures, especially the most vulnerable and defenseless. Between my love for plant- based foods and cruelty free makeup, I emphatically believe that improving animal welfare standards will lead to a more empathetic world. As a woman whose mission is making the world better, I'm over the moon that I get the opportunity to interview and write about the most discernable, clear-sighted women in the world, who inspire me so profoundly.

This imbues my mission to rescue the sweetest most fragile creatures . . . like the day my friend and I encountered a lost, terror-stricken, adorable, white poodle who narrowly missed getting

THE BOOK ON GRATITUDE

hit by a car and returned her to her sobbing, grateful owner.

Another time, while driving with my boyfriend to a ballroom event, I was feeling like royalty in a lovely short-flared dress with a fitted bodice and strappy stiletto heels. As we drove toward the Marriott, there was a baby kitty on the side of the road, her ribs horrifically showing, gnawing at a plastic bag! People rushed right past her not noticing at all. Forgetting that cocktail hour was fast approaching, and we were going to miss it, I hurried toward the emaciated, sickly-looking, meowing kitten with gentle eyes pleading for help. Today, she is in the most loving home, bringing solace to her grateful owner who has fallen so in love with her, that she has a social media page for her with tons of followers!

As another example, I even risked being fined in a sleepy little NJ town when I fed an abandoned kitty. Even though I knew I was violating a city ordinance, I could not spurn this pitiful creature and I fed her anyway! So, when I ended up in court with thousands of dollars in fines, the judge asked, "Why are we punishing her for doing something in her heart she knows to be right?" I was tickled pink. What a conquest! Nadia Comaneci's words, 'I can do it on my own!' sang in my ears.

The fines were dismissed, and I found more kittens loving homes. May my example encourage others to step up fearlessly and do the right thing.

My fervent hope is that animal-loving celebrities will each donate a million dollars to local animal rescue groups and charities. This money will go a tremendous way to mitigate their unnecessary suffering.

Every day, I am grateful for my fellow animal rescuers. However, it is much more than that. It's for the affable co-existence of all living beings, in the purity of all sentimental hearts, that there is forgiveness in love stories, that in goodbyes there is still hope, that change is inevitable and even in our murkiest times love is palpable, insightful, probing, and obtainable. Love is always how we survive. May God bless your precious fur baby, your cherubic little newborn baby, and you! ✯

Barbara Blue

Barbara lives with her daughter, DeAnna on The Wild Atlantic Way, in Connemara, Co Galway, Ireland. Both are native Gaelic speakers, which is only common in a few tiny pockets of Ireland called a 'Gaeltacht.'

Barbara has a BA Hons degree in English and Irish, from NUIG College, Ireland. After college she spent a few years in Milwaukee, US, and returned to Ireland working in the world of accountancy and finance. She completed an online Diploma in Psychology and Counselling — where she got in touch with her 'inner author.' Barbara then, spent a few years writing scripts for a long-running Irish speaking (Gaelic) soap drama called Ros na Run, on top of her full-time finance job. Barbara has participated as a co-author in our previous two bestselling books in the Inspired Life Series: *The Book on Joy* and *The Book on Transformation*.

When Barbara is not avidly reading as many books as she can, she loves to cook, watch movies, and spend quality time with her friends and family.

Contact
Email: babsblue@gmail.com

The Biggest Gift of My Life

By Barbara Blue

"Being grateful does not mean that everything is necessarily good. It just means that you can accept it as a gift."

— Roy T. Bennett

For me, the above quote is currently quite poignant. Very recently, I received the biggest gift of my life — the gift of a permanent home. After decades of paying rent, of struggling financially as a single mother, and as someone who never thought I'd see the day I'd call myself a homeowner, this gift is literally beyond adequate words of gratitude for me — even while I'm overwhelmed with the feeling and the emotion of it! Being a homeowner now means security for me and my daughter. No more packing up and moving away if a landlord decides to sell the property. No more putting effort into making somewhere a home, even though it will never be my own and I don't know how long I'll be living in it. No more stressing about where we might end up in five years' time, or what I'll even be able to afford by then. It oftentimes still feels surreal to me, as the magnitude of such a gift is almost too much to process. I think it will take some time yet for it all to sink in, but I do know that I will be eternally grateful for something so utterly amazing and life changing.

Did this gift come at a price? Indeed, it sadly did, as it came through the death of my much-loved father. We had already lost our mother 11 years previously, so Dad was left as our anchor, our confidante, and a best friend all round. It didn't matter how often we visited him — each visit always meant a huge hug and kiss on arrival and again on departure. I loved how after his big hug goodbye, his scent would linger on my own clothes for a while so it felt a part of him was with me for my journey home. I miss those hugs more than words can say. Dad was someone you could laugh with, cry with, or just be yourself in any capacity with. He was a rock for us after losing our wonderful mother, as well as our beloved brother. He was a doting grandfather to my daughter (his "sweethearteen" as he always called her), and when she was a toddler, they would spend many hours 'traveling the world on exciting adventures' together . . . albeit through vivid imagination from his boat that was grounded beside the garage!

> *"If the only prayer you said was thank you,*
> *that would be enough."* — Meister Eckhart

Losing someone you love dearly is a most difficult thing to endure. It can often take time to start filtering through the haze of grief before the joy and gratitude start to shine through — gratitude for having someone so amazing in your life to begin with, and for all the memories you got to share together. In this case, not only do I get to experience the gratitude of having had such wonderful parents, but I get to inherit their legacy of the happy home they built together and raised us all in. It is a legacy full of treasured memories and an abundance of love. It is a home where I can only hope to continue creating more memories, as my own legacy to pass on in time to come.

> *"Let gratitude be the pillow upon which you*
> *kneel to say your nightly prayer."* — Maya Angelou

Although I believe myself to be somewhat spiritual, I am not a religious person. I'd be more of an agnostic who does believe in a spiritual 'realm' of sorts, without believing in one particular religious sect or order. I recall a time that Dad and I went to see a medium. I had tried fortune-telling before so expected this to be along the same lines. I had quite a bit of skepticism about the whole thing — although probably not as much as Dad did! It wasn't too long after my brother had committed suicide, and we were all left with so many unanswered questions and 'what-ifs' and horrendous grief.

Without going into all the details, all I can say is that both Dad and I were a bit shell-shocked leaving the place. Mom, Ciarán (my brother) and many others all came through for us both, with clear specific details that could never be guessed at or known to any others apart from themselves. It was a bittersweet experience, in that we shed a lot of tears but were also so happy to hear from them, and the whole thing was a real rollercoaster of emotions. The main thing I took away from it, is that it seems our loved ones really do linger with us and watch out for us, and have no suffering of any kind anymore. It's something that gave me a lot of comfort and which I feel hugely grateful for.

My prayers now consist mostly of a chat to my deceased relatives, or any other good-natured powers that be, asking that they keep those I know and love, safe and happy. I always add a thank you to them — for their protection and continued love. So even through the heartbreak of Dad passing away, I was truly grateful to know that he would now join the spiritual ranks of so many wonderful friends and family members and continue to be with us.

As well as being grateful for those no longer with us, it goes without a shadow of a doubt that we also should feel hugely grateful for the people still around us who bring happiness to our lives! To take any of these people for granted would be at the cost of our own joy. We should always carry the awareness of how much these people mean to us, and feel the relevant gratitude in accordance with same.

"Let us be grateful to the people who make us happy; they are the charming gardeners who make our souls blossom."
— Marcel Proust

I personally feel grateful every day for the abundance of incredible people in my life. I'm grateful for my wonderful daughter who I'm proud of and love dearly. Grateful for my amazing friends, who help brighten my every day. Grateful for my lovely family, who have all pulled together in love and support throughout the recent transition of losing our Dad, as well as for many years beforehand. I thank all of you for being my 'charming gardeners!'

> *"Acknowledging the good that you already have in your life is the foundation for all abundance."* — Eckhart Tolle

My wish for you is that you feel the joy and happiness that comes with acknowledging and being grateful for everything good and positive in your life. And that for anything bad or negative in your life, you can feel grateful for the experience and the inner-strength you might find to get through.

I thank you for taking the time to come on this journey of gratitude with us!

THE BOOK ON GRATITUDE

Notes

Victoria Chadderton

Victoria Chadderton is an author, trainer, speaker and Distinguished Toastmaster. She works with transformational leaders training, facilitating workshops and retreats. She is an Amazon Best Selling author. Her work with the Law of Attraction has brought out her passion for helping others visualize and obtain what brings them JOY!

In addition, she has been active in local community organizations, such as Boy Scouts of America, Washington Elementary PTSA and Women's Service League. Currently she is the District Director of District 9 Toastmasters. Victoria lives in Washington State and enjoys spending time with her family, going on family vacations and exploring new places.

Contact
Website: www.victoriachadderton.com
Email: chadderton.victoria@gmail.com

Magical Moments

By Victoria Chadderton

"Enjoy the little things, for one day you may look back and realize they were the big things."

— Robert Brault

His face lit up with excitement. In the distance he could see his favorite character. "Pooh, Pooh" he yelled. Winnie the Pooh could not hear him as he was busy on the other side of the bushes interacting with another family on the patio. My grandson had waited with excitement and anticipation from the moment he learned that we were going to Disneyland. There were discussions daily of what we would do, what characters we might see and what was Disneyland going to be like. To be there, in that moment and watch him experience the magic I will be forever grateful.

So many times, we are asked or think, "What am I grateful for?" Most people answer like me and will go immediately to the major milestones (moments) in their lives.

I am grateful for my children, for graduating college, watching them get married, becoming a Nana and many other huge moments in my life. I am grateful for these memories as they play a major role in how I continue living my life. I am grateful every day that I have my children, that we live close to one another, and we get to share many magical moments as a family.

From a very young age, I knew that I wanted to be a mother. This desire might have come from the fact that my mother and I had a rocky relationship. She had envisioned what she thought a mother-daughter relationship would look like. I had my thoughts of what a mother-daughter relationship should be. However, they did not match up. From the beginning, my mother and I were at odds. We never saw eye to eye; we viewed the world through different lenses. She loved fashion, glitz, and glamor. I ran around in jeans and a t-shirt playing in the mud.

My parents adopted me at birth and brought me home from the hospital and began our family of three. We lived near my grandparents for the first five years of my life. I was close to my grandmother. She understood me. We would bake and tend to her garden and flowers. We took walks around the property and enjoyed each other's company.

When we moved to Los Angeles, California, 2,258 miles away, I missed the strong connection with my grandmother. We visited at least once a year. My grandmother would fly to see us occasionally. However, my favorite was going back to my grandmother's house, which I always considered to be home.

During the 1984 Summer Olympics, my mother sent me to stay with my grandmother for the summer in Washington State. I was 14 at the time, and my mother was a single working parent and felt that I would be safer with my grandmother.

This was one of my favorite summers. My grandparents lived on a ranch and kept ranchers' hours: up early in the morning, big meal at noon and evening was spent reading and chatting about the day. I enjoyed baking biscuits and cookies. She even taught me how to can jelly that summer. I am grateful for all the little moments of baking and conversations. I did not know at the time that the summer of '84 was going to be the last time for these magical moments. My grandmother's health declined. She passed away as my father and I were driving up to Washington to be with her. Looking back, I treasure all of those together times.

Occasionally, my father would take me to Disneyland for the day. I loved the magic of walking through the tunnel and seeing Main Street, hearing the music, and smelling all the wonderful aromas. As a teenager that became one of the hangout spots for me and my friends. My mother did not go. After she and my father divorced, she would get a friend of hers to take me. However, I finally got her to go one time with me.

Disneyland has been a special place for me since an early age.

I took my kids to Disneyland's 50th anniversary Christmas 2005. There was lots of celebrating. My mother was living in California at the time, and we lived in Washington State. I told her we were going to Disneyland for Christmas, and she was welcome to join us. She hadn't seen her grandsons in over a year and took me up on my offer. I bought her a train ticket, and we met her at the Anaheim train station. We had magical moments on that trip that my boys still talk about. Her one and only ride was the Indiana Jones Adventure, and when Pluto startled her and she screamed from fright.

Family has been important to me all my life. I am grateful that my sons grew up living close to one set of grandparents. Other than a few years that my mother was in California, she lived close to us, and I always encouraged the grandparent/grandchild relationships.

As my mother's health declined and her last moments drew near, a rush of emotion came over me. She had been in hospice for a few weeks. This was the last time that I could be with her and say anything that I wanted to say. I felt as though she had waited until it was just the two of us. My father had left the room, and I was sitting by her side, holding her hand. I told her that I was going to be ok. She no longer needed to hang on to be there for me. I told her I was understanding what motherhood was like and all the feelings and emotions that came with that role. We all make mistakes (or what we feel are mistakes) in parenting. The look in her eyes as she took her last breath is one that I will never forget. Dying is one of those events that we are unable to give an exact time until the moment it happens, just like birth.

We were not together for my first breath. I am forever grateful that I was able to be with her for her last breath.

There are so many moments in my life that I am grateful for. Both moments of joy as well as moments of sorrow. I strive to learn from all of them. My mother's passing has been one that I think of often, and it is a great reminder that we never know when we will be able to have those discussions with the ones we love.

Last year my father and I were having a rough patch in our relationship. He was 89 years old, and his health was not the greatest. He was making decisions that I felt were not good for his age and current health situation, but in the end, it was his decision on what he wanted to do. I disagreed and could sometimes respond with a curt answer because I was annoyed.

One night, as I was getting ready for bed, my father asked how my day was. For the past few weeks, I sounded snippy with my answers, so I took a deep breath remembering that life is made up of many moments. We do not know how important a response at the time could be. I said my day went well, that I was tired, and ready for bed.

He smiled and said, "Love you."

I looked at him and said, "Love you, Night." Those were the last words we said to one another. He died in his sleep that night.

I am coming to realize how important all these moments are in my life. I am grateful for the moments I have experienced and learned from. I am most grateful for all the magical moments that are still left to create. I am looking forward to all the excitement and joy I see when I watch my grandsons experience something new. I will treasure all the future family shenanigans. I have decided to list all the moments big and small that I am grateful for. I invite you to do the same.

What am I grateful for? I am most grateful for My Family . . . Mi Familia!

THE BOOK ON GRATITUDE

Notes

Cherylanne Thomas

Cherylanne's passion for life has her living in the fast lane where she is most comfortable. She is a bestselling co-author and has received her MBA and several certifications focused in the area of Sales, Marketing, Executive Coaching and Leadership Development. Cherylanne serves as a senior sales and marketing executive specific to the hospitality industry and has worked for many luxury hotel brands including Ritz Carlton, Waldorf Astoria, and Hyatt Hotels and Resorts.

For the past 25 years, with curiosity and passion to elevate sales and leadership teams to a higher level of performance, Cherylanne has transformed organizations toward greater success by discovering what works to increase their topline revenue. Cherylanne is a distinguished Toastmaster who has authored several white papers on luxury marketing, success principles and service excellence. She is a bibliophile, an avid sports enthusiast and volunteers in her spare time to local pet shelters. Originally from Boston, Massachusetts, Cherylanne currently resides in Nashville, Tennessee.

Contact
Website: www.cherylannethomas.com

The Discipline of Practicing Gratitude

By Cherylanne Thomas

> *"In the past, I always thought of gratitude as a spontaneous response to the awareness of gifts received, but now I realize gratitude can also be lived as a discipline. This discipline of gratitude is the explicit effort to acknowledge that I am and all I have is given to me as a gift of love, a gift to be celebrated with joy.""*
>
> — Henri Nouwen

I believe gratitude is a spiritual virtue. It helps us love more deeply and be present to our divinity at work in the world. Practicing gratitude has numerous benefits including positively affecting our physical, mental, emotional, spiritual, and relational health.

According to Dr. Robert Emmons, a leading researcher on the topic, there are three stages of gratitude: 1) Recognizing what we are grateful for, 2) Acknowledging it, and lastly, 3) Appreciating it. In other words, appreciation is the final component and the last stage in the gratitude process; it is a building block for the culture of appreciation.

It has taken me most of my adult life to receive gifts of praise and help, in the spirit of love, gratitude and joy, mostly because I did not feel worthy. It is only in my recent years that I have come to believe that gratitude is a conscious discipline that brings me closer to my divine creator, and to the life and people around me.

Not too long ago, I was watching a featured segment on the TODAY show and they introduced the founders of Hidden Gems Literary Emporium: Kaila and Raymond Sykes. Hidden Gems Literary Emporium is a donation-based bookstore that gives out thousands of free books every month. Their philanthropic mission touched my heart in such a special way that I was compelled to demonstrate my gratitude and I donated over one hundred books to support their cause. I never gave my gesture any further thought once the books were sent; it was simply my small way of expressing my gratitude for the mission they drive forward every day.

Time passed and one day I received a piece of mail from Hidden Gems Literary Emporium. I assumed that it was a receipt for my donation. Instead, it was a thoughtful and touching hand-written note from co-founder Kaila Sykes. The note went into specific detail and provided examples of how specific books I donated touched the hearts of people that frequented the Emporium. She ended her letter by thanking me for the many ways I spread joy to people all around the world by co-authoring two international bestselling books.

This considered act of care and kindness came full circle for two strangers because of my watching a TV segment. I expected nothing in return. Kaila's gratitude came back to me tenfold as I was in gratitude to her and her family for creating this unique and generous non-profit that touches so many lives. I consider this non-profit organization the manifestation of a gratitude discipline.

It was because I was mindful and aware to take action in the moment, to sharpen my powers of observation, to notice what others may have missed, and thus to discover more layers of richness in an ordinary life, that I experienced this special engagement with a total stranger. This is a proven example that gratitude absolutely matters.

A thankful heart breeds contentment. My thankful heart is content for seeing so many gifts of life itself. A thankful heart promotes optimism. Did you know that optimism leads to enthusiasm and determination? I know this to be true, and I live it every day. A thankful heart brings healthy attentiveness. It finds time to slow down and count blessings. A thankful heart shifts the focus of attention from us to others. It humbly realizes it has benefited from others and as a result is more apt to notice others' needs. I suggest that you contemplate this way of being for your own life's enrichment. Practicing such gratitude consciously brings me closer to God and his people in so many random, rewarding ways.

Another thought I have is that gratitude heightens the enjoyment of the good seasons of life. It also provides strength to make it through the difficult seasons as well. However, gratitude can be finicky. There are seasons of life where gratitude is easy, whereas at other times, it remains elusive. When the storms of life hit—as they inevitably do, gratitude may not come so quickly. It is hard to be thankful when our world is crashing down. Yet, those are the days we need it most; those are the seasons of life when it is strength, optimism, and perspective that will carry us through.

During a very painful and dark time of my life, I took care of my late husband, Jor, by providing 24-hour care when he fell terminally ill with a deadly disease that took his life in a matter of a few short months. I felt so blessed and in gratitude that I was chosen to care for him and have him die in my arms Yes, I was in pain and my heart was broken, but I was not angry or bitter. I was in a space of deep gratitude to have been chosen to help transition him with love into his immortal world.

Gratitude requires practice when it is easy and even more practice when it is difficult. In addition, the more we train ourselves to that end, the easier we can access it when we most require it.

> *"Be intent upon the perfection of the present day."* — William Law

Finding good is always around us, even in difficult times. How often do you take time to reflect on the many good things in your life that you may have rejected or ignored? It may be conversations you were too busy to have, unnoticed smiles, gifts you neglected to share, or simple pleasures and graces gone unnoticed. By contrast, how often do you complain about something? When you complain, you affirm the opposite of what you want.

It is my belief that it is our responsibility to share with others. Having a daily discipline of gratitude offers our grace to others freely and generously with a sense of joy and no expectation of anything in return.

At its core, a gratitude practice is about paying attention, noticing, and naming the gifts of blessings that surround you. The most common way to do this that I have found is to live a conscious life. Having a daily discipline of gratitude enables me to live richly, offering to others what I can give freely and generously, with love and grace.

To me, gratitude is a frame of mind, a way of seeing the world. I personally have made it my discipline to practice gratitude throughout each day. I notice that it affects my life and those around me in such a positive way.

> *"Gratitude bestows reverence, allowing us to encounter everyday epiphanies, those transcendent moments of awe that change forever how we experience life and the world."*
> — Sarah Ban Breathnach in Simple Abundance

Developing a discipline of gratitude is essential for us as we grow in our knowledge of God and our experience of him. Perhaps thinking of gratitude as a spiritual discipline is a new idea for you. Growing and continuing in our spiritual formation means that we need to continue to expand our thinking of what spiritual disciplines are. There is the discipline of surrender, the discipline of listening and the discipline of gratitude.

I believe gratitude is an awakening to our sense of dependence on a higher authority and others; life cannot be rewarding without such gratitude. I also believe that gratitude is the byproduct of something we cannot produce ourselves. Gratitude happens when we experience grace, and it happens with regularity when we understand grace. Grace is present when we hear a heart-felt thank you. Simply saying "thank you" is a very different thing, however. "Thank you" requires us to recognize that someone did something good for us. Grace is also present when we see and feel the wondrous gifts around us and take pause to be in gratitude. For example, when I simply inhale a breath of fresh air into my lungs or notice the geese that march by my patio each morning, I feel God's grace and it fills me with joy and gratitude.

Why is the discipline of gratitude so important? Why must I cultivate this disposition in my own life? My belief is that gratitude is an interactive spiral between the giver and a receiver. It recognizes that a gift of exchange has occurred. We thank the giver with an expression of appreciation. A gesture of gratitude completes the circle and lets the loving act flow from giver to receiver and then back to the giver again. I elaborated on this earlier describing my experience with Ms. Sykes.

The discipline of gratitude means we are practicing and producing an attitude of being thankful, even in those moments when we cannot appreciate what we have. This is an aspect of how our higher power has benefited our lives. This also has a relational application. It helps us with others as we actively demonstrate our support, appreciation, and compassion to them for how they have benefited our lives.

Implementing the practice and discipline of gratitude, will unmistakably and massively boost your contribution to the world and to those around you. Based upon that, you will live a life that matters. I am living proof. ✺

JAN FRASER INSPIRED LIFE SERIES

Inspiring
GRATITUDE

Robin Eldridge Hain

Robin Hain had a thirty-year career with Colgate-Palmolive Company, managing $10 million annualized retail sales. Her strong project management and team building skills consistently achieved growth initiatives.

Her B.S. degree in Psychology, served as a strong foundation for her continued pursuit of best practices in mental health, substance use disorder and trauma recovery. Robin serves on the boards of www.MWVsupportsrecovery.org and www.sicd-fl.org raising funds and awareness in her community and enriching her knowledge of recovery challenges and opportunities. Robin's experience with teaching and collaborating, coupled with her innate ability to give and help others, allows her to impact the world in an incredible way. She is a gifted author in the Inspired Life Book Series and her chapter in this book is dedicated to her husband, Scott, whose partnership sparked mutual growth and dreams fulfilled. They reside in Sarasota, Florida and Silver Lake, New Hampshire, enjoy traveling and cherish time spent with family and friends.

Contact
Website: www.robineldridgehain.com

When One Plus One is So Much More Than Two

By Robin Eldridge Hain

"At times our own light goes out and is rekindled by a spark from another person. Each of us has cause to think with deep gratitude of those that have lighted the flame within in us."

— Albert Schweitzer

My spark was ignited on an airplane by a blue-eyed man with the gift of ease in conversation. What I observed was his sincere desire to engage with others that shared his space, to find common ground and make a connection for that moment or a lifetime. Immediately, I realized he had the characteristics of the man I wanted to spend my life with. Previous to this moment, I endured a brief unhappy marriage, when I was 28 and thought I was ready for that step. After two years of introspection and identifying qualities I desired in my life partner, Scott, the blue-eyed man, was clearly the one for me.

Being specific when you set your goals is critical because you will get what you ask for — for better or for worse.

JAN FRASER INSPIRED LIFE SERIES

I set out to capture our 30 years of marriage in a 30-page Shutterfly Book which evolved into 44 pages. And that was only the good times. It's the good times we capture with photos. It's our response to life challenges that seals or breaks bonds. In my case, our love has grown stronger with each day we share together in sickness and in health. Turning the pages of the joys in our life I cannot overstate my gratitude for the life we have shared.

I have found that when you are on the same ship going in the same direction everything is possible. One plus one is so much more than two.

When I contemplated writing a chapter in "The Book on Gratitude," I knew my chapter would be dedicated to my husband, Scott. The strength of our love allows us to spread our wings individually and together. Our friends and family have multiplied. Through the years many dear people have transitioned beyond this life. To those that have passed the memories we made together are sealed forever in our hearts. New friendships continue to evolve as our shared interests and new experiences expand our journey through life.

Looking for the perfect home was one of our first adventures. We kept coming back to a white cape cod with grey shutters in need of lots of tender loving care. The dogwood trees, azalea bushes, and daffodils were in full bloom surrounding the sylvan pool filling the backyard with the potential for relaxing family weekends. Right from the start we activated an annual home improvement plan. Our house was our hobby for twenty-five years. Scott would handle structural challenges and I would paint and decorate. Our homes have been a magnet for family and friends to gather throughout the years. We enjoy entertaining and creating spaces for laughter and healthy memories.

Travel became a priority when I became a grand prize winner in a $10,000 Quaker Oats Sweepstake from a 25-cent cereal coupon redemption. This amazing trip started at the Sonoma Mission Inn and Spa where massages, seaweed wraps, manicures, pedicures, and healthful gourmet meals rejuvenated us beyond belief. The correlation between self-care and success became very clear to me. Ah! if I could only carve out time and space for this type of pampering, how could I not be successful in life! Following five nights, falling asleep in our king size down cloaked bed in view of a romantic fireplace glow, we checked out with a $5000 gift certificate for a return visit. We explored Napa and Sonoma wineries. We traveled north through the Redwood Forests into Mendocino and south from San Francisco to Los Angeles. Over gourmet dinners it came to us: travel expands your mind unlike any other experiences. The excitement and joy of meeting new people added new places to our bucket list. We returned to the Sonoma Mission Inn & Spa the following year on our way to Honolulu. My sales team at work won the top prize of one week in Hawaii for exceeding our sales goal.

Family vacations became a priority as we caught the travel bug. Sail-boat charters out of Newport, Rhode Island and Tortola, British Virgin Islands brought our family closer together. Setting sail early in the day allowed ample time to explore the treasures of each port in the afternoon. The fresh air and the rhythm of the boat drifting on the mooring provided restful sleep for all.

A shift in the economy slowed commercial construction which afforded Scott an opportunity to complete an accounting degree and work as a private assistant to an investment banker friend he had known since his childhood. This new position came with an added perk to oversee his boss's home in Carmel, California. This led to our introduction to Clint Eastwood, at his Mission Ranch Restaurant, where he stood larger than life with a serene smile and a strong handshake. Exploring Carmel-by-the-Sea and coastline of California with our family was a perfect respite for many years. The giant seals slept on the shoreline as we approached Hearst Castle in San Simeon. We started our National Parks tours with Yosemite followed by Yellowstone, Grand Tetons, Grand Canyon, Monument Valley and Arches National Parks. Oh, the wisdom of Theodore Roosevelt in creating the U.S. Forest Service to protect the gift of these lands.

The Outer Banks, North Carolina called us back two years in a row. We shared a week with three families and our respective three generations, fishing, swimming and building sandcastles. In Costa Rica, Scott, Nevin and I zip lined, rode ATVs and went scuba diving, the first time for all of us. Vacationing with our children was all about sharing new experiences, building bonds, and memories to last a lifetime.

In a flash, our children became adults. Parenting to two sons and a daughter through significant milestones in their lives strengthened our bond. We celebrated their successes and we stood by them during turbulent times. They came with their own destiny, their own dreams, and their own method to execute their life plan. The grandchildren now bring us spark and joy. We are grateful for the time we share with this new generation.

We celebrated our Silver Anniversary on a small sailing vessel off the Amalfi Coast. A two-week Riverboat Cruise from Budapest to Amsterdam expanded our friendships around the world. Machu Picchu, Galapagos and Alaska awakened us to how minuscule we feel occupying these vast lands filled with history beyond our imagination.

> *"Feeling grateful or appreciative of someone or something in your life actually attracts more of the things that you appreciate and value in your life."* — Christiane Northrup

One plus one is so much more than two.

Take the time to see each other. Really see each other. Look, listen, share. Strengthen the core of your relationship as you reach out to the world. When challenges arise, hit them head-on with a compassionate heart. Let the space between you be a table filled with a feast of possibilities as there is often time not one, single solution, but an assemblage of ideas to contemplate. Look, listen, share, respect and you will witness the expansion of the universe.

Every day I count my blessings and express gratitude for Scott's love and partnership. Our journey is a combination of charted courses and out-of-the-blue storms.

When life shifts us off-course, we lift each other up and follow the stars to find our way home. ✹

THE BOOK ON GRATITUDE

Notes

Cindy Stewart

Originally from Northwestern Pennsylvania, then transplanted to Missouri, Texas and North Carolina, Cindy calls Kernersville "home". She is a Diploma RN (St. John's School of Nursing) followed by a BSN (Southwest Missouri State University); and a MBA/MHA Degree (Pfeiffer University). She is certified in Healthcare Quality, the Canfield Methodology and Train The Trainer Professional Development trainer. After 37 years in a variety of healthcare nursing roles, she decided to be her "own boss". As a successful business owner, she knows firsthand the impact joy and gratitued have on lives.

An avid volunteer, she is involved with SistersHOPE.org, Kernersville Friends of the Library, Crisis Control Ministry, and the Kernersville Chamber of Commerce. Her words to live by are: FAITH, FAMILY (includes friends) and FUN.

Her purpose: encourage individuals to creatively DREAM BIGGER & DECIDE WHAT they want out of life!

Contact
Email: cindystewart250@gmail.com

Gifts of Gratitude and Quiet Joy

By Cindy Stewart

"There is a calmness to a life lived in gratitude, a quiet joy."

— Ralph H. Blum

Connection. Community. Comfort. Calm. These simple words inspire me daily to live a life in gratitude.

In the first book in the *Jan Fraser Inspired Life Series, The Book On JOY*, I had the privilege to write the chapter "Scatter JOY", reflecting on the words by Ralph Waldo Emerson.

Now in the third book of the *Jan Fraser Inspired Life Series, The Book On GRATITUDE*, I am again honored to share a few personal moments and stories in my life that actually connect lives of family, friends and the Kernersville Community. This time, the chapter **"Gifts of GRATITUDE and Quiet Joy"** encourages you to pause and reflect on the moments and the people who come into to our lives. Hopefully after reading, you too will be inspired to share how you choose gratitude as a daily part of your life. How gratitude influences your dreams, your life and your stories.

It was December 2017 during the holiday season. Christmas has always been an exciting time for our family and friends. Each gift carefully selected. Gifts exchanged. Unfortunately, or fortunately, several of the presents for me had a waiting period. The gift from my husband was a week-long training experience to take place in August 2018. My daughters, knowing my favorite childhood movie, gave me two tickets to the live production of "The Sound of Music" scheduled at the Durham Performing Arts Center for April 22, 2018. I was ecstatic. Funny, my husband did not care for musicals and encouraged me to ask a friend to go along. Plans were made and I anxiously awaited the days for both events to come.

Four months later, fast forward to the week leading up to the Sunday performance on April 22, 2018 (Earth Day), my husband had been traveling. We had a full weekend. Friday was a fundraising event. Saturday was a full day at the soccer fields for John, and I was preparing for travel to enjoy my Christmas gift from the girls. Sunday began early at 6:30am, since John had to be at the soccer fields and I had to get in the holiday spirit. With a gentle kiss on the lips, we said our goodbyes as we planned to see each other for dinner around 6:30pm. Then mid-morning, I realized the performance time was not a matinee, but an evening performance. My last text to John was to let him know of the change in plans and I would see him later that night.

The performance was exceptional. Immediately prior to intermission, tears filled both my daughter and mine eyes and those all around us, as Mother Superior sang "Climb Every Mountain". Of course, after the musical, driving home down Interstate I-40, I was singing all the songs from the musical at the top of my lungs. Imagine that! What a wonderful gift. I was so grateful to attend the performance and share the experience with my youngest daughter.

Upon arriving home after 11:00 pm, I called out, "Honey, I'm home." No response, however, Monday morning's trash was in the middle of the kitchen and the basement lights were on. John was tending to his normal chores. Again, I shouted down the basement. I was home and proceeded to the bedroom to don my nightgown and prepare a cup of tea. I knew I was not going to be able to sleep anytime soon, endorphins were flying high. I texted my daughter I had arrived home safely.

THE BOOK ON GRATITUDE

Then realizing I had not seen my husband, I went into the basement and found him lying in the garage, not breathing. A call to 911 nor CPR did not bring him back to me. Kernersville's finest policemen arrived minutes later. The officer in charge, Sean, was kind and soft-spoken. He was training a new officer to the force and asked if I would allow the training officer to interview me. As a former nurse educator, who trained and mentored new graduate nurses and experienced nurses, I was grateful to participate in his training. This provided me with a sense of peace. After John's body was taken away, the officer asked if he could take out the trash from the kitchen for me. Although I declined his offer, he insisted. Small acts of kindness make such a difference in our lives. In my heart, I believe his death occurred during the song prior to intermission. I also believe the joyful ride home after the performance in the dark of the night gave me strength to endure what was to come. Family and friends provided unbelievable support and an outpouring of love to my daughters and me.

Quiet joy! Connection. Community. Comfort. Calm.

August 2018 arrived and John's Christmas gift to me from 2017 was a ticket to Breakthrough To Success seminar in California. As an avid longtime follower of Jack Canfield, renowned author and speaker, I knew I was meant to meet Jack. My husband knew how important this was to me and he knew what I wanted to do for the next 30 years! I wanted to give back to the nurses and my community by sharing and spreading the gift of *The Success Principles* as a Canfield Trainer. I am forever grateful knowing that John supported my dreams, even in death.

Quiet Joy! Connection. Community. Comfort. Calm.

Fate would bring the young police officer, Sean, and I together again in the Spring of 2019. It was during my time as a participant in "Leadership Kernersville" sponsored by the Kernersville Chamber of Commerce. For extra credit in the program, we were permitted to ride-along with a police officer for a shift. I selected a night shift. The sergeant on duty was preparing introductions. Both the officer and I looked at each other, smiled and knew immediately no introductions were necessary. We had met previously in April 2018 late on a Sunday night in my home. Yes, Kernersville's newest K9 officer, Sean, was my assigned officer for the night. Grateful to see each other and know how each of us were doing was a gift. We had ample time throughout the shift to get reacquainted, including the opportunity to catch up on family happenings and I experienced firsthand a K-9 in action.

Quiet joy! Connection. Community. Comfort. Calm.

In February 2021, I marveled at how lives can intersect and one might not even be aware until days or months later. One of our community resources is an alert email system, keeping citizens appraised of different events and happenings. I am a recipient of such emails. On this early Sunday morning, I drove to pick-up a fresh cup of coffee for my mother and me. While driving back to the house on the phone speaking to my sister, I witnessed a sudden flurry of activity. Police sirens blaring and lights flashing. I stopped and watched as the police cars flew by. I announced to my sister, "Something really bad must be happening in Kernersville." Upon arrival at the house, I shared the activity with my mother. Then I read the email alerting people to stay indoors (Oops! Too late.) and that a police officer had been shot.

My mother and I immediately began to pray for the officer, rosaries and all. I lit a candle for his healing and safekeeping, which burned all day. Over the next 48 hours, I had not heard further news of the officer. However, I met a friend who was in "Leadership Kernersville" with me. She and I were discussing our day and things we had to do. She mentioned taking items to the Chamber of Commerce for the family of the officer who had been shot. I had not learned of the officer's name until that point, it was my Sean. I burst into tears, knowing our past connections. My thoughts immediately going to Sean, his wife, his children, and other family members. The Kernersville Community rallied around the Police Officer and his family. Community events and fundraisers popped up overnight. Grateful for the chance to give back to the one person who made a tremendous difference during a very difficult day in my life. Now I could return similar support.

Quiet Joy! Connection. Community. Comfort. Calm.

Time for reconnection arrived in November 2021! An exciting time of the year occurred at the area-wide Annual Awards Banquet. As a member of the Kernersville Chamber of Commerce Board of Directors and Executive Board, I attended the banquet and was pleased to see Officer Sean. He had made a remarkable recovery after numerous surgeries. It was an extraordinary opportunity to celebrate Officer Sean as he received the "Citizen of the Year Award" for his service, heroism and contributions made to our community. " . . . A walking miracle" was cited in the *Kernersville News* to describe Officer Sean. After the banquet, I took the opportunity to speak with Sean, his wife, and his parents.

I was grateful for the chance to say, "THANK YOU," and witness how our lives have crossed paths over the years.

I have chosen to live a life of gratitude and quiet joy. Will you join with me to choose this for your life?

The rewards are boundless.

Quiet Joy! Connection. Community. Comfort. Calm.

Joy Bach

J oy graduated with a Journalism degree and minor in French from the University of Wisconsin. Since then she has worked in advertising, radio, television and event planning in Milwaukee and Chicago. Joy is a writer, marketing professional and musician. She has sung in intimate venues from The Blue Bird Café in Nashville to singing in front of thousands for pro sports teams and festivals like Summerfest, the world's largest outdoor music festival. She leads a few bands in the Milwaukee and Chicago area.

Over the years, Joy co-founded several organizations, including the Filipino-American Student Organization at UW and the community-based nonprofit Libertyville Health and Mental Wellness north of Chicago. She serves on several boards, including Craftsman Café, a philanthropic organization that brings together musicians and builds community while serving charities across the Chicago area. Joy will always have her hands in different projects and continues to travel the world, as she believes it is the best way to stay engaged and be an eternal student.

Contact
Website: www.joybach.com

Hardships and Blessings

By Joy Bach

"If you look for the bad, you'll find it. But if you look for the good, you'll find it. When you look through the lens of love and gratitude, you will find both become good."

— Joy Bach

As I lie in bed fiddling with my phone, I hear her down the hall. The already busy shuffling of her slippers and low humming of a Frank Sinatra tune, I wake with comfort knowing she is near. Her armored frame may be tiny but houses the might of a warrior with the calm confidence of a life well-lived. Most would never know what a privilege it is to be in her presence. I do.

Many of the beautiful lessons I learned from my mother come from the gift of gratitude. She has lived a life of tragedy and joy, poverty and wealth, unconditional love and sorrow. One thing remains steady — her faith, love and gratitude.

I recall one night falling asleep to the soothing cadence of my sister's inhale and exhale. Mom was baking *pandesal* downstairs and the scent of the fresh bread floated from the kitchen, up the stairs, into our rooms. I slowly climbed out of bed and quietly toe-heeled down the stairs to see Mom working in the dark kitchen with only the dining room pendant light on. I asked her to tell me a story as we waited for the *pandesal* to bake.

Mom smiled, obliged and began, "*It was dusk. We could hear the Japanese bullets in the back of our house. It was an open field of rice paddies . . . pik-boong . . . and then we could hear the Americans retaliate . . . rat-tat-tat-tat-tat . . . The police came to our house and said the fighting was coming closer; it was time to evacuate. We traveled at night and stayed hidden by day, so we would not be seen from above,*" Mom said, sprinkling bread crumbs on the rolled dough.

"*There is a river we crossed during the war. I can still remember the undertow pulling me downstream. I held on to my dad's arm so tightly to stay afloat. I looked around and saw the long lines of families trying to cross too.*" In my mind, this river that Mom referred to many times during my childhood seemed like a babbling creek. As an adult, I had the opportunity to stand right at the edge, looking at the vastness of this "river" in bewilderment and wondered how anyone could cross without a boat.

Mom stared off, replaying a film of memories and shook her head. A smile slowly formed, "*What a childhood. So many interesting experiences. I am so thankful.*"

Riveted, I soaked in her story. I thought of the fear she must have felt in those moments and how her family came together during their greatest test of faith. And what struck me most in her reflection — she was thankful.

Over the years, other stories would surface. Growing up in poverty, Mom soon had to choose her vocation. Education is the epicenter of pride in the Philippines and provides the hope of financial success to be able to support the family back home. Nursing was the perfect option for Mom. When Mom was struggling looking for employment, her aunt happened to be in town and told her about an American program called "Operation Brotherhood." Mom left all that she knew and joined a team of nurses in the villages of Vietnam and Laos.

"*When I joined Operation Brotherhood, we saw cases where patients hadn't received medical help in years. We flew in planes, sitting on the floor, strapped to the side of the plane like cargo. One night, I remember waking from a dead sleep, hearing shouting and seeing nurses flee as the roof above us was collapsing. Could you imagine?"* she asked in awe. *"What an adventure. We were so grateful to the United States for giving us nurses that opportunity."*

Again, I heard her wrap the story with that word: gratitude. What I did NOT hear was a complaint. Not once. Mom lived through true hardship, found goodness in patience and reaped the rewards of a deeper, meaningful life. Then said, *"Thank you . . . for all of it."*

I reflected on her life and wondered how she found the grit to rise to these challenges. How did she face fear and overcome adversity? Some people may have given up, become hardened and ask, "Why me?" But not Mom. Weathering these storms taught her patience and developed a quiet strength, humility and perspective. At the center was her strong faith. Her deep prayer is what pulled her through. Seeing every hardship as a trial worth enduring was grit and trust that God had a plan. And the fact that Mom saw every situation — the good and the bad — as a blessing, that was gratitude.

I think of the times that I struggled in my life. The times where I was in the midst of darkness, where I felt rudderless, ashamed or hurt. Mom would advise, *"See your pain as your charity. Pray to fill your heart with more love. Do not choose hate, anger or fear. Choose love, hope and trust. Put it in God's hands and let it go."*

Her positivity was a choice she made every single day. Her faith, love and gratitude was her way to surrender and accept each situation as lessons and gifts, blessings for which to be grateful. I looked at my life and asked how I have incorporated these beautiful tenets into my life? What have I done to look for the good amidst the bad? How do I practice gratitude and give back to those in need?

I remember sitting on the family room steps crying to no one. It was a time in my life where I was questioning my purpose and direction. Previously, I worked in a fun creative environment where my co-workers became dear friends. I made the very important decision, and happily did so, to stay home and raise our children. Somewhere along the way, I had lost my identity. I went from feeling needed and important, to washing clothes and doing dishes. I was turning 40 years old a year or two later and wondered what did I have to show for my life? Thinking of my mother, how she navigated her thoughts, her energy and positive outlook, I looked inward and asked, *"So what are you choosing to do about it?"*

I got busy living. Instead of looking at what was holding me back, I started taking inventory of what was possible. What were my interests, what were my skills and what problem was I trying to solve? I prayed for guidance and direction. I thought of Mom at 42, trying something new and getting her driver's license. It motivated me to begin blogging about *Trying Something New* on a weekly basis. Leading with love and gratitude, I jumpstarted my life and started to reclaim me.

Committing to researching and writing about a new task each week led me to some amazing feats and more importantly, dynamic people. I learned how to fly a helicopter, snowboard and surf. I wrote about catching Adele early on her "19" tour at an intimate Chicago venue, learned weaponry as a Black Belt, sang with a Broadway star, collaborated with a designer and created a line of leather goods, played sous chef to *Top Chef's* Stephanie Izard for a night. I took an improv class at Second City, wrote my first song (en francais) and ended the year taking the polar bear plunge in Lake Michigan on New Year's Day. I also gave back by paying it forward to strangers — Starbucks for a mom and her kids, Panera for a Marine. I visited the elderly and painted a home with Habitat for Humanity.

Leading with faith, love and gratitude, I was open to where this passion project would lead, which included being a frequent guest on a local morning show. I had no idea what God had in store for me, but He taught me to take a low point and turn it into a highlight of my life, reminding me of the adventurous spirit my mom had. I flipped the bad into good.

But it did not stop there. As I continued to look for the good, the opportunity came to join a medical team of doctors and nurses headed to the Philippines for mission work. I said 'yes' and joined them for a life-altering journey. It came full circle for me as I accompanied friends and colleagues of my father, who had passed away a few months before I got married. Starting the week taking photos as a historian, I ended the week scrubbing in and assisting in removing a tumor from a woman's breast in the operating room! I spent time with these doctors who used to come over to play tennis during the day and poker at night. Seeing them in their element while giving back was a privilege. I listened to their stories between the jokes, beers and karaoke. In spending time with them, side-by-side, I learned more about my dad's life and the respect they had for him. He was a mentor and helped them start their practices. I felt closer to my father and realized he was a man before he became my father. This trip was yet another blessing in deep, meaningful ways.

I thought of both my parents on the plane ride home and how they chose to rise to the occasion versus folding to the difficulty. They chose to sacrifice versus taking the easy way out. They appreciated the process versus complaining about the inconvenience and taught me that how we perceive every situation, decision and relationship is a choice. If we choose to be thankful, we train ourselves to look for the silver lining. This means that no matter how we were raised or what experiences may have altered our path, we have a hand in life's outcome.

Being thankful is a practice that transforms us from victims to victors of circumstance.

I returned home and took inventory on how good life was. I experienced some eye-opening epiphanies that recalibrated my life. I loved my kids better. I had deeper conversations and felt closer to my husband than ever before. Most of all, I was looking for the good. Any worry or roadblock was overcome by faith, trusting there was something better to be unveiled. Love and gratitude were abundant with each person I was honored enough to meet and learn from.

Ten years later, I found myself sitting on my friend's floor talking about what the next chapter holds. We talked about how legacy does not have to be one big epic thing. It is the 10 little things we do throughout our days and how we impact others that matter. How do we love? How do we treat people? What are we grateful for?

These questions inspire me to practice gratitude every single day. It may be starting and ending each sunrise and moonrise with a "thank you for . . .". I practice looking for the good and celebrate the small wins like picking the right security lane at the airport, the thank you wave from letting someone go before you, the belly laugh of a child.

Whispering "thank you" throughout the day changes the tone of our mood, our day, our perspective. It changes how we interact with others and moves their hearts a little towards love on the continuum. And when we are filled with joy and gratitude, we spread our light and help others find their light, joy and gratitude.

Take inventory, friends. Look for the good things. And think of Mom who reframes hardships to blessings. Look for the lessons. Lead with love and ask yourself, "What is good? How do we love? How do we treat people? What are we grateful for?" ✹

Notes

KDB Wheeler

KDB (Karmen De Bora) Wheeler was not expecting a stroke to change the trajectory of her Executive and Leadership Coaching business at the beginning of 2021. She found herself relying on her most trusted strategies when her life was jolted by a life-threatening medical event. It was these strategies that helped her survive and transform her experience into a positive and successful outcome. KDB used her vivid story-telling skills to rewrite the narrative of recovery. KDB has been coaching executives and leaders in both the public and private sectors over the past decade. Her unique certifications include George Washington University's Center for Excellence in Public Leadership e-Co Executive Leadership Coaching, Barrett Values© Centre Certified CTT Consultant and Leadership Embodiment© certifications, the University of Santa Monica's LM&SCL II certification, and she is an International Coach Federation® certified PCC coach. KDB graduated *magna cum laude* from National-Louis University with a Bachelor of Science in Management.

Contact
Website: www.kdbwheeler.com / Email: 7Tools.kdbw@gmail.com

Finding Gratitude in Trauma

By KDB (Karmen De Bora) Wheeler

"How you relate to an issue is the issue [just as] how you relate with yourself while you go through an issue is the issue."

— Drs. Ron and Mary Hulnick

When a major trauma occurs in your life, the last thing on your mind is "I am so grateful for this!"

Gratitude comes from the Latin word *gratus*, meaning "pleasing, thankful".

When a blood vessel burst in my brain on January 22, 2021, *gratus* was not exactly the first word used.

It was more like "expletive deletes" that followed the realization my left-side didn't work at all, and the right-hand was unable to figure out how to operate the mobile phone. My brain registered, "I need to contact someone" — preferably Fire Department Emergency Medical Services (911).

Then I realized right-hand coordination was limited to redialing the last phone number called before noon. I thought, "Hopefully, they answer." My stomach felt queasy. I forced myself to stay awake.

"Hopefully, they aren't in a meeting." I felt faint. "Hopefully, they will contact 911 for me." They answered!

I then thought, 'Hopefully, the EMS Team will get me to the nearest hospital's Emergency Room in time for ER professionals to administer TPA medication to help restore blood flow to my brain with the hope of preventing severe stroke damage.'

They did and it did! I faded into unconsciousness and woke up in the Intensive Care Unit. I realized my left side was paralyzed — face to toes. Back to waves of nausea, as a cloud of horror began to envelop me.

Everyone deals with personal disasters differently, and I became horrified at the prospect of being confined to a wheelchair. I wasn't mentally ready to embrace rotating care givers helping me in and out of one.

I was especially grateful to learn my prognosis presented the other side of 'hopefully,' as in 'recovery sooner than later.' Possibly not to pre-stroke-levels, but I could get close.

Relating to this issue (stroke recovery) with myself, while going through the issue (all the therapies and re-education) was the issue. Time and focus became critical to shifting my relationship to all of this.

It doesn't matter the size of the blood vessel that bursts — where or on which side of your brain it happens — your life will be impacted. Routines will be disrupted. Comprehension, speech, mobility, strength, and dexterity become distant goals in a long process of relearning, and I was one of the lucky ones.

A sense of gratitude began to slowly replace the horror. Notice I didn't say 'instantaneously.'

To be able to move forward with my recovery, it was better to mentally give up — aka relinquish this type of horror. That, or get sucked under in a debilitating, emotional riptide.

The counterpoint was being in awe of synchronistic and fortuitous events that popped up around me like wildflowers and bushes pushing their way up through asphalt. Law of Nature reminder: wildflowers and bushes always prevail!

After I was released from the ICU and my week in a step-down unit was coming to an end, the next location was an In-Patient

Rehabilitation Center. Who knew there were so many facilities specializing in traumatic brain injury recovery? There were numerous choices in the region where I lived. Who knew choosing one of these would be like trying to choose between a four- or five-star restaurant or hotel? Hey, I was just trying to get a little In-Patient Therapy already!

One such synchronistic event was when the hospital Case Manager was someone known by the friend who answered my phone call to contact the EMS Team. Knowing this hospital person turned out to be a *fortuitous introduction*, especially after my initial conversation with the Case Manager at the Rehab Center.

I learned quickly that unless you're physically or cognitively **unable** to help yourself, and you require assistance, the expectation is you will handle making all post-stepdown-unit arrangements.

I dutifully phoned the number provided and was informed that the length of stay, and all therapies would be approximately 10-days, and then sent home. Then three-days-a-week In-home Therapy. Are you kidding me?!

I paused and asked, "You **are** looking at the correct patient — right? You do see that I'm paralyzed on the left-side, right? As in, can't walk, have no arm or hand functions, can't speak or swallow properly, am in a wheelchair and need 24/7 help? So, would you please explain how all this is going to 'get fixed' in 10-days?"

The response went something like, "You go home and, if you fall down, you can always be re-admitted."

I exclaimed, "I can do WHAT??!"

When the hospital Case Manager followed up with me to learn the outcome of this conversation, you can imagine her shock and disbelief with the information conveyed to me. She promptly offered to make all arrangements on my behalf. I was fortunate to have such an accommodating person assigned to me, as not everyone experiences similar hospital staff responses in these situations.

This was my first opportunity to express immense Gratitude for help above and beyond standard care.

Once I was successfully installed at the Rehab Center, my weeks were filled with daily schedules of Physical, Occupational, Speech, Recreation, and Music Therapies. While grateful to have so much focused care five- and six-days a week, I had imagined a less rigorous schedule. Sometimes, I had to laugh at myself. Just how did I think I was going to improve rapidly with part-time therapies?

When frustration threatened to set my mindset back a week, I acknowledged Gratitude for the small steps achieved. This practice definitely stopped mental and emotional downward spirals before the negative mind-chatter got totally out of control.

Another practice I used was to express daily appreciation to the teams of professionals caring for me. An **Attitude of Gratitude and Appreciation** for everyone, from the housekeeping staff to dining services, from med techs to phlebotomists, and everyone in between. These times were all opportunities to practice **what I teach**.

Yes, the TPA medication saved my life, and I was grateful that any possible brain damage was contained. It was the side-effects of this medication that were shocking to me.

Once again it was a real stretch to feel grateful when experiencing any of these: bleeding from puncture sites and wounds; difficulty breathing or swallowing; headache; nosebleeds; paralysis; and prolonged bleeding from cuts.

None of the medical professionals conveyed any of this to me — from the ICU to the Rehab Center.

I did my own research when no one could explain why blood arbitrarily oozed from my mouth as though I was screen-testing for a part in a remake of the movie *Dracula: Dead and Loving It*, or why the nosebleeds rivaled the mouth bleeding. You get my point.

I was grateful that my sense of humor was still intact as these side-effects and their momentary drama would launch my carefully crafted **Attitude of Gratitude and Appreciation** straight into a medical waste container.

On a different note, the face and mouth paralysis I experienced had me in gratitude overtime because I could still essentially talk, chew and swallow.

Talk: haltingly at 1st, then at 2nd — there was no 3rd <joke>, as my brain did its best to transmit words to my mouth to construct requests and responses.

Chew: very slowly at first, trying to figure out how to get my brain to send correct signals to tongue, teeth and jaw to make this happen.

Swallow: continuously difficult for the first 12-plus-months as the left-side paralysis wore off. While the movements required new-found coordination and patience, these were all so much easier when learned the first time around!

Despite being able to do all three of these functions post-stroke, I spent the entire first four months being thoroughly annoyed with my new levels of competency. (Or should I refer to it as "incompetency"?)

My choice of relating to "these ongoing frustrations" became a model to practice **what I teach:** *how relating to myself while going through these issues **was** the issue.*

How many of us are presented with opportunities to re-imagine our life after a traumatic life event (especially a medical)?

What course of action would you take if this unique scenario put you at the imaginary intersection of "No way it's happening" and "This can't possibly be me."

While I absolutely do not advise having a medical emergency to begin using this almost magical transformational tool: *How you relate to an issue **is** the issue.* By incorporating Gratitude into my day-to-day interactions with folks I came into contact with, I was able to "leverage my privilege for the privilege of others", as the saying goes. Having opportunities to express my Thanks! to anyone contributing to my recovery, made certain that I stayed focused on outcomes and the people helping me achieve them — not inconveniences of the moment.

Have you ever met someone who was dead set on staying stuck on some position (or opinion) because they were certain it was the other person's or institution's fault? There weren't enough facts or information to the contrary that were going to shift this person's perspective. Whether positive or negative, their position was 'The Only Valid One.'

Or they misinterpreted what was said, and created a mental (or emotional) story of what just happened? Now they are hurt, angry, surprised — fill in the blank — because they were certain their version of the story was the correct one. Whether positive or negative, their version was 'The Only Relevant One.'

Not to say I was initially successful every time, but I deleted "staying stuck" from my vocabulary as soon as it was physically, mentally, and emotionally possible. Notice I did not say "instantaneously" here either.

Working on relearning simple physiology of walking, talking, swallowing, breathing, using my left arm and hand all required help from others. And I gratefully accepted it all!

I was on the recovery ward for three months where I met several patients who were adamant their lack of positive outcomes was the fault of — fill in the blank. These positions somehow came to also include family and friends who'd come to visit. Not really sure how that was supposed to work, but it sure was entertaining to watch the debates.

There were other patients who became outraged that various staff had somehow been less than professional in their dealings with them, or weren't listening, or paying proper attention to them, or whatever the slight was. From my seat in a wheelchair, these conversations definitely sounded like a misinterpretation of what was said.

Have I expressed yet how much entertainment value there is in hospitals and Rehab Centers? Not that I'm recommending you get Box Seats to a Recovery Unit Production. <big laugh> When I focused beyond the pain, depression, inconveniences, et al, there was a very comedic side to my day-to-day activities.

Ultimately, I appreciated both my sense of Humor and Gratitude. They were how I *related to the issue of stroke recovery.*

These practices and tools, combined, have saved my life — from sanity to well-being. **I now teach them**, and five more, to others.

It is always immensely gratifying to hear success stories from my clients through their use of one or more of these tools.

It is my wish, should you ever find yourself seeking ways to refocus, adjust and/or renew your spirits after a traumatic experience, that these practices and tools will help you with your recovery. No wheelchair required. ✵

THE BOOK ON GRATITUDE

Notes

LouAnne Hunt

---※---

LouAnne is a Canadian Keynote Speaker whose down-to-earth humor compels audiences to laugh while they learn. After thirty-six years, she retired from her government job. A second career in teaching the fundamentals of Business to thousands of adult students as a College Professor allowed her to polish her presentation skills. She has made a name for herself as a sought-after speaker, teacher, and Personal Development Coach.

Additionally, LouAnne is an award-winning entrepreneur, putting into practice what she teaches every day. She is a Certified Canfield trainer in *The Success Principles*™ and Diabetes Prevention Program Lifestyle Coach. As of June 2022, she is a #1 Amazon Best-Seller in 7 categories for her contribution in *The Book On Transformation*. Her latest project as TV and radio talk show host for *The Mindset Playground* can be found on Youtube and BoldBraveTV.com. If you are interested in having LouAnne work with you, in a group or as a motivational speaker, connect with her through her website.

Contact
Website: www.louannehunt.ca / Email: louanne@louannehunt.ca

Dad's Legacy

By LouAnne Hunt

"Any man can be a father, but it takes someone special to be a dad."

— Anne Geddes

Do you believe in serendipity?

On April 1, 2011, I was working with my friend at the Home and Leisure Show. We had a booth, and we were selling great products to the show attendees. Directly across from our booth was a home generator booth with three men. It was Friday and as we waited for the next crowd to shuffle in one of the guys from that booth came over to our booth and started chatting with us.

He asked me a lot of questions such as: was I single, if I had kids and where I worked? Just the normal personal questions you would ask to get to know someone. He was friendly and handsome but as he walked away, I noticed he had a wedding ring. What?! His questions were personal and, in my opinion, should not come from a married man. At that time, I had been a widow for four years and hoping a new guy would come along . . . my handsome prince.

What I didn't know is that the married guy was asking me all these personal questions and going back to his booth and relaying the information about me to his partner. He was encouraging him to make the trek across the aisle and meet me. Shortly after our chat, his partner built up enough nerve to walk over to me and extended his hand "Hi, I'm Dave." He literally had me at "Hi."

We started talking and . . . (here's the Serendipity part) realized we were at the same event six months earlier in Michigan when I was invited up on stage to tell my story. I talked about becoming a widow and Dave was in the audience listening to my story. He told his friend that my story moved him and that he wanted to meet me to hear the end of my story but there were so many people around me, we didn't get to meet.

Six months later, we were now face to face and during our conversation Dave realized I was the girl that was on stage in Michigan, the girl he wanted to meet. So, as it turned out, it was six months later that I met my Handsome Prince, my soulmate and my best friend.

I am grateful for meeting Dave. I knew I had met the father I had always dreamed of when I met his dad.

My life as a young girl seemed lonely. My parents were divorced when I was three years old and my brothers lived with my biological father while my sister and I lived with my mother. Because my mother worked and I had no father-figure in my life I was alone a lot and I became a dreamer. This was an amazing life lesson because I learned independence. I learned that I am capable of taking care of myself and I became successful in my life by making the right choices. I especially learned that I am enough, that I can be on my own and thrive.

I surrounded myself with great friends and many of those friends became my family. I so appreciated my friends, but I always yearned for that father-figure. A girl's daddy is the most important person in her life and that was missing in mine.

Shortly after we started dating, Dave introduced me to his mother and father. I immediately felt a bond with them both and called them Mom and Dad. Most of the family referred to them as grandma and grandpa.

Dave's dad was born in 1927 in the same farm house in the country where he lived most of his life. When I met him, he was 84 and I

THE BOOK ON GRATITUDE

was amazed at how young at heart and active he was. He sang in two men's choirs, one at his church and a community choir that traveled locally and entertained audiences. The first time I met him was at a small church where they performed for an audience and I was literally blown away by this performance. At the front of the church was a massive organ with pipes running from the back of the organ to the ceiling. The sight was breathtaking seeing such a historic piece in this small church. Each member of the choir was dressed in a crisp white shirt, tapestry embroidered vest and a black bow tie. The sound that came from that choir gave me chills. Dad loved to sing and he had an amazing voice.

I loved visiting with Dad every chance I could. There were family dinners at restaurants, at the farm house in the country, picnics by the lake and church events. He loved ice cream (any flavor would do), even if he was full from a meal he would laugh as he told us 'there is always room for ice cream.' Opposite to his favorite, he had a fear of snakes. He told us about the time that he was riding his bicycle and a snake had sprawled out across the end of the driveway basking in the sun. He didn't see the snake until he almost ran over it with his bike but as soon as he noticed the sun bather, he dropped his bike on the spot and ran in the opposite direction. The snake may have been harmless but he wasn't going to stick around to find out.

Every month an event known as 'Pie-Day' had the church parishioners gather to make apple pies and raise funds for the church. Dad's job was peeling the apples. There was a kitchen tool that did the heavy lifting but it was his job to make sure the apple was sitting perfectly on the tool to peel the apple upon cranking the handle. At the same time, it gave Dad pleasure to gather with his friends from the church.

He was quite handy and could fix just about anything. During Dad's lifetime he was a bee keeper, welder, builder, farmer, and raised cattle, pigs and chickens. On many occasions, we would drive through the nearby town and dad would point out the houses that he built or helped to build.

Dad was a farmer through and through. One summer day when I was visiting him at the farm he was sitting at the picnic table writing in a small notebook. Being an avid journal keeper, I asked him what he was recording in his notebook. "I do this every day," he said. He explained, "I write down the weather, temperature, wind speed and direction." I looked at him with a raised eyebrow 'wind direction?' "You have to know what direction the wind is blowing to know if it's ok to spray the crops or your spray could end up in the neighbor's field," he stated.

Dad was a historian and loved to tell stories of his childhood and family. We had many dinners at our home on Sundays and we would ask him about what the world was like when he was younger. It was like we were sitting around an old radio when he would share one of his childhood memories.

Dad told us about the school he attended, "Down the road at the corner by the lake stood an old school house where the area children were taught grade one through eight." Dad was one of those students and he would walk down the dirt road for one mile to the little school house.

In 1937 an agricultural class at the school received a gift from British Royalty, King George VI and Queen Elizabeth (known by our generation as Queen Mum) during a Canadian visit. The gift was three acorns from an oak tree on the royal estate at Windsor Castle. One of the acorns was lost from the package. The other two acorns were planted into a small pot and kept in the window of the round room attached to the school house and carefully tended by the students. In the spring one of the acorns sprouted. The students continued to watch over the sprout and watched it grow into a healthy tree. Dad along with a dozen classmates planted the young tree near the road and today the tree has grown to be a sturdy, regal British oak tree. It was designated as a historical tree and cannot be touched. A bronze plaque was erected to identify the tree and remains at the site though the school house was torn down years ago.

I am grateful that I finally had the Dad that I had dreamed about and hoped for my entire life. I loved hearing his stories and we were able to spend many hours together. I told him over and over how grateful I was for having him in my life even if it was only for a short time. I told him that he was the Dad I had always wished for as a little

THE BOOK ON GRATITUDE

girl. I wrote several articles for a local magazine. Dad was a fan as I shared those magazines with him. He would read the stories many times and then pass them along to his friends to enjoy. I only had him in my life for ten years and seven months but during that time, we shared a deep admiration and appreciation for each other.

In November 2021, Dad passed away. COVID was still rearing it's ugly head and we were advised at the funeral home not to expect many for the visitation due to government restrictions. Amazingly, we had more than 400 visitors come and pay their respects. It just proved how special Dad was in our community.

The day of the funeral was a beautiful sunny day and many people attended the outside ceremony at the cemetery. Music recorded by Dad and his choir rang out across the cemetery grounds. Directly above where he was laid to rest, a tiny rainbow appeared briefly peeking through the clouds as if he was sending us a final farewell.

When I came home from the funeral, I wrote this entry in my Gratitude Journal:

On November 6, 2021, my special Dad passed away. I am so grateful I had him in my life for ten years and seven months. He was such an incredible dad.

I will miss our talks about his childhood, I will miss his stories, I will miss his generosity. I will miss his thoughtfulness, I will miss his singing. I will miss his Joy (things that he loved). I will miss our dinners out and take out. I will miss his childlike amazement at modern day things like our cell phone. I will miss his support of me and my business, and I will miss MY DAD.

Thank you for answering my prayers and bringing a Dad into my life. ✺

Linda Rose Jensen

Linda Jensen has been licensed in the financial services industry since 1994 and is committed to maintaining the highest standards of integrity and professionalism. Linda is a Certified Financial Educator and a SOFA Financial Literacy Instructor. She has conducted regular seminars for the public and business professionals on a variety of topics for the past 24 years. She specializes in retirement and income planning as well as tax planning, long term care planning and estate planning. Linda is a holistic fiduciary financial planner who always has her client's best interests at heart. She is passionate about helping her clients create a successful retirement with an emphasis of avoiding the many risks of retirement.

Linda and her husband Brad met in college. They enjoy the Pacific Northwest and are proud to call it home. They love spending time with their children and grandchildren. Linda is a life-long learner who enjoys reading, hiking, cooking and sewing.

Contact
Website: www.heartfinancialgroup.com
Email: linda@heartfinancialgroup.com

There is Always Hope

By Linda Rose Jensen

"Normal is just a setting on your dryer."

— Patsy Clairmont

Two words summed up my childhood: fear and confusion. The root of the fear was because both of my parents were mentally ill. Dad was violent, and I thought mom could kill me by looking me. I was the oldest and had three younger brothers. I was the responsible one who would take care of the kids and tried to pick up the mess. I learned to cook when I was young. No role models, just a kid trying to figure out how to make things work. No one knew what life was like. I had no words to describe the chaos. I had some friends, but I was limited in terms of spending time with them. I never invited them to our home. We figured out mom's mental illness years later after my sister-in-law was diagnosed as borderline personality disorder. My youngest brother is a very talented neurosurgeon. When he was in his psychiatric rotation in medical school, I begged him to figure mom out. Instead, he married her likeness. There are different types of borderlines. My mother was the queen who could behave like a witch. My fear was extreme. I consciously wanted to be invisible.

Part of the confusion was because life was so unpredictable. I never understood what would set them off. This was my biggest mystery as a young child. When I was an adult, I realized that mom would instigate dad's violence. She was a master at pushing his buttons. She didn't dish out the physical abuse, but she was really good at shoving him over the edge. Borderlines live like the world revolves around them. They can suck the oxygen out of a room. Mom didn't allow any privacy. She didn't think it odd to come into the bathroom when I was on the toilet. Once I came home from school and she had thrown everything in my bedroom out the 2nd story window. My life was in the yard. Dirty and broken. It was humiliating having to pick up the things that were precious to me.

The best thing that happened to me was when I was in kindergarten. A girlfriend invited me to a Good News Club. That's where I heard the Gospel. One time and it stuck. I understood that God loved me and wanted a relationship with me. Imagine, the God of the Universe loved me! There was no love at home. We were a bother. We were poor. We were to be seen and not heard. But I learned to pray and depend on my relationship with God and His precious son, Jesus, to manage and cope through the experiences. That decision was a game changer in my young life.

I was barely 18 when I started college. I had been sheltered and was shy. This was quite the experience. I met my husband a couple of months into my freshman year. He was 19. Gosh, the guy was crazy about me. To this day, he is still deeply in love with me. I don't understand it, but I am so grateful. He's my best friend and soulmate. One of his roommates, a psych major, gave him a paper to proofread. It was about the effect of mental illness on a teenager. Brad gave it to me to read. I couldn't stop crying. That was the first inkling for me to try and put the puzzle together. I had really believed that everything was my fault. I had so much guilt that I really didn't understand why I was still alive.

By the time I finished my sophomore year, I knew that I didn't want to spend that summer at home. I was on my way to make some semblance of my life. When I told my mother of plans to live with Brad's grandmother until school started, she was angry. In an effort to resolve the conflict Brad drove me home. Mom wasn't there when we arrived.

When she did arrive, she didn't say a word but simply walked across the room and slapped me hard across my face. I just stood there and didn't blink. Brad got me out of there quickly. He was amazed at my reaction. I think by then I was numb.

Mom threw me out like the trash. I had no contact with my little brothers who I loved and missed sorely. I was really depressed because Christmas was coming, and I wouldn't be able to see them. I remember the dark and lonely place where there doesn't seem to be any light or a way out. It reminds me of a dream that I had for years growing up. I was coming home from school and had to cross a huge canyon. It was so wide that I couldn't see the other side and so deep that I couldn't see the bottom. I had to cross a rickety wooden bridge. Every time I got to the middle of the bridge, I would fall and then wake up. Years later I described this to a therapist and told him that I didn't understand the meaning. He said: "That's simple. You would rather fall into the abyss than go home."

Wow, that made total sense. Amazing what your subconscious can dream.

I decided to commit suicide. I was 19. No one knew, not even Brad. I took an entire bottle of pills. I didn't care about living. I wanted to escape the pain. I felt that I wasn't important and that there was no reason to keep living. Brad called. He couldn't understand my slurred speech. He came over to the apartment and found me passed out. He was able to get me to the hospital in time. My stomach was pumped out. The doctors and nurses were kind. Brad told the police that I made a mistake taking the pills so that I didn't end up in a psych ward. *He didn't realize that I deliberately took all of the pills.* Brad saved my life.

When I reflect on this experience, I am so grateful for Brad and his intervention. The reason is that I have so much to be grateful for. We grew up in the Northeast. I lived near Philadelphia and Brad near New York City. We met in college near West Point. Because we were so young when we got married, we have grown-up together. Both of us were tired of living in such a fast-paced culture. When we left, I described it as a rat race. AND the rats were winning! I wanted to move out West, but Brad wanted to move to the Florida Keys. So that's what we did. Most folks move to the Keys when they are retired, but we were young adults. We bought a home on a canal. We had a boat on our dock. One direction into the Atlantic Ocean and the opposite was into the Gulf of Mexico. Brad had his electrical license and started out working for contractors. After a few years, he went into business.

Our children, a son and daughter, were born in the Keys. What a life! When the kids were small, I'd clean the house in the morning and then take them to the beach or the pool. Sometimes we would visit daddy on a jobsite. Brad specialized in new construction. The Keys are a hundred miles of islands and bridges. We were club members at a 5-star resort and would spend time at night and on weekends there swimming and enjoying the amenities. We were hours away from Miami and about an hour from Key West. Pretty isolated. Instead of farmland, we had the ocean. Life was laid back. The most popular tee shirt was, "It's 5 o'clock somewhere." Tourism and fishing were the main industries. I used to say the retirees were the 3rd industry, 'transfers of payments,' meaning their Social Security and pension checks. Brad used to say it was 99% alcoholics and the other 1% were heavy drinkers. Not too far off . . . But it was paradise to us. Life was sweet.

When our son was in 3rd grade, I was really concerned about all of the drugs in the Keys and how the kids were affected. I thought our son was pretty smart and wanted him to have a better education. Brad and I decided to leave. I talked him into visiting family in the Pacific Northwest. We made a few trips without the kids. Over the summer when our daughter was nearly 5 and our son finished 3rd grade, we moved to Washington State. What an adventure. Moving from the Southeast to the Northwest part of the country, corner to corner. We started over.

Brad took a few months off to study and take the Washington State electrical exam. He was hired by a large contractor and for the most part handled the estimating. After 5 years, he got a job with the State as an electrical inspector and eventually worked in the plan review department, approving the plans of schools, medical facilities and prisons.

When we arrived our daughter, Kathryn was starting Kindergarten. Kristan would begin 4th grade. I had always wanted to become a financial planner and got a job with Prudential Preferred. Today our son is a particle physicist. He's married with three little boys. Our daughter has her Master's in Education and is a stay-at-home mom with two young girls. Brad is retired now. He is a watercolor artist, makes violins and is now learning to play the pedal steel guitar. Would you believe it has two necks, ten strings per neck, eight-foot pedals and five knee pedals? It's the most complicated instrument I've ever seen.

The Keys had gotten boring. It was just hot and hotter. No change in the seasons. We absolutely love the Pacific Northwest and Puget Sound. There is so much to do. British Columbia is a few hours away to the North. The Cascades and Olympic Mountains are fairly close. The Oregon Coast is a couple of hours south. Such beauty to enjoy and never tiring. As I mentioned, I grew up near Philadelphia and I thought the Poconos were mountains until we moved out West. The weather is moderate. Snowfall is measured in feet, not inches. For the most part it stays in the mountains where it belongs.

This was definitely home for us. We still go back to the Northeast for visits, but we would never want to live there. We absolutely appreciate a much better quality of life.

In a couple of months, I'll be starting my 29th year as a financial planner. I've been an independent advisor for more than 25 years. I'm passionate about the industry and financial literacy. I love helping my clients create a successful retirement. I'm an educator at heart and it's a perfect fit for my passion of problem solving. I tell clients that I'll be sick or dead before I quit because of how much I enjoy helping them.

Behind our home is a State Forest. It's 10 minutes to the freeway or shopping. There's a wonderful State Park connected to our neighborhood. I love walking the trails. It's so beautiful any time of year. The vegetation, bunnies, garter snakes, snails, ducks, geese, and the occasion eagle. The salmon run in November. There's a creek running through it and wetlands. It is God's cathedral.

What I am attempting to describe is the life that I love. Brad and I have been married for decades and decades. We have two wonderful children and five grandkids. We enjoy each other more and more as time passes.

When I think of my suicide attempt, I can't help but think of the wonderful life I've had as well as the privilege of spending it with the love of my life. Through all of my experiences, my children, the grandkids, and the places where I have lived, I'm grateful to have celebrated a long and happy, healthy life. Not that there aren't challenges. That's the way things are. But challenges can bring opportunities for growth. We always need to remember that our situation doesn't have to stay the same. There's always a solution to the problems that come up. I believe that all of us have a hole in our heart that we stuff with something. We can put an addiction into that hole: drugs, alcohol, sex, or pornography. Maybe religion gets stuffed in that hole. For me it's God that is in my heart. He guides me, comforts me, gives me peace, and I desire His wisdom most of all.

I live with gratitude for my life, my family, my business and my relationship with God. I choose to live expectantly and look for blessings with gratitude for the present and trust of the future. I believe that gratitude = joy!

THE BOOK ON GRATITUDE

Notes

Ilka V. Wilson Vallee

Ilka is a #1 international best-selling author of several books and a fervent leader with an extensive track record for helping individuals, communities and organizations transform and reach their highest potential. She is a lover of people and life and is dedicated to mentoring and guiding people and organizations to identify and activate the leader within. She is a strong believer that following God's design is the perfect blueprint for authentic leadership. Her goal is to awaken the masses and help them create and lead a life they love living every day.

She is the President of Corporate GOLD LLC, a leadership consulting, training and coaching company. She is a certified emotional mastery, life mastery, and transformational executive coach, and an international inspirational speaker. She is passionate about leadership, transformation through trusting the process and leading in excellence. Her slogan is "Learn It, Live It, Lead it!"

Contact

Websites: www.ilkavchavez.com / www.corporate-gold.com
Email: Ilka@corporate-gold.com

The Power of Leading with Gratitude

By Ilka V. Wilson Vallee

"The power of gratitude is that it yields grace."

— Ilka V. Wilson Vallee

Ephesians 4:29 — "Do not let any unwholesome talk come out of your mouths, but only what is helpful for building others up according to their needs, that it may benefit those who listen."

Gratitude is defined in the dictionary as the state of being grateful: Thankfulness. Appreciate is defined as to grasp the nature, worth, quality, or significance of or to value or admire highly.

Gratitude is the most powerful feeling any leader can express and appreciation is the highest feeling any employee or subordinate can feel. Our words and actions, what we say and do as leaders can inspire gratitude and appreciation or it can inspire ingratitude, feeling of unworthiness, or lack of appreciation.

Imagine this is the incredible power you exude as a leader with your words and actions.

Some have long term impact on those that you lead. I remind you to consider what legacy you are currently leading and where change may be required. Busyness, the burden of leading, lack of learning to remain present, distractions, and life's demands may be culprits in you forgetting to be grateful or even saying thank you for a favor or job well done. We even overlook adding the word *YOU* to the word Thanks. The word *YOU* adds meaning and power to your expression of gratitude. As a leader, how often do you take time out to personally thank your employees or even members of your family? To be present and genuinely thank someone, where they can feel your gratitude heart to heart. With the influx of social media, it is easy to focus on what others have and take your eyes away from being grateful for what you do have.

In a Glassdoor survey, 81% of employees said they would work harder for a grateful boss. I wonder if lack of gratitude is attributing to the mass exodus of employees from the workplace? Gratitude is important at work, in the community, and at home. To simply choose to appreciate instead of depreciate takes effort. Gratitude is not something to be taken lightly. Some may think why should I express gratitude when someone is being paid to do their job? This may be an attitude expressed by both leaders and customers alike. One may lose sight of someone operating in excellence despite being paid because they are focusing on the monetary exchange instead of the demonstration or shining light on the company's values, mission, or vision. That the individual may not be simply doing the job assigned but is going above and beyond to model the foundation of the company or values that their family established at all costs.

> "And be thankful . . . with gratitude in your hearts . . ."
> — Colossians 3:15-17

Gratitude is an essential skill that every leader must possess. It costs nothing yet is still underutilized. It could simply be starting your day with gratitude. It can change how you treat the first person you see that day. It changes your focus. It drives you to a place of gratitude and grace rather than ingratitude and lack of grace.

I recall starting in a new position. I grew up in a culture where you greeted everyone you saw with Good Morning, Good Afternoon, or

THE BOOK ON GRATITUDE

Good Evening, depending on the time of day. Every morning I would run into the same man at the elevator and I would say "Good Morning" and he would never reply. I decided after a while, that I would continue to say "Good Morning" despite his lack of acknowledgment. I realized that I was able to continue this without taking it personally because of the genuine gratitude I felt for seeing another day.

I share with you that my persistence paid off. After one year, he finally began replying "Good Morning." After sometime, we became good friends. I realized that he was so caught up with work probably before he stepped on the public transportation that he probably did not have the capacity to acknowledge my salutation. Most likely, he never paused to express gratitude for the things he had as he worried about what was to come in his day.

The power of gratitude is real. Although I was unaware at the time that gratitude is what kept my salutation consistent and genuine. It paid off. Gratitude has the power to reverse mindsets, feelings, and emotions. It impacts your quality of life and that of those you lead.

My definition of leadership is aligning your values with your actions, words, and the way you live and inspiring others to do the same to make the workplace and the world a better place. Why not start your leadership with gratitude. I recently read a devotional by Pastor Rick Warren who introduced a term entitled *Radical Gratitude* which I love. He said *Radical Gratitude* means you're going to walk through life being grateful in every situation, no matter what — in times of plenty, when times are tight, when times are good, bad, right, wrong, whatever. You can develop an attitude of gratitude by choosing to be grateful in every situation. The attitude of *Radical Gratitude* actually serves others; it becomes a ministry." Wow, imagine if every leader adopted this attitude of Radical Gratitude? Of being grateful through the good times and bad. Pastor Rick said, "There's power in leading with gratitude, because the followers know that all things will eventually work out for the good of everyone who loves the Lord and is called to his good purpose." There is grace attached to gratitude. A grace that surpasses all understanding and reminds each person of their worth, their truth, and their power.

People can improve their gratitude habits. It can be nurtured or starved. The decision is yours. I leave you with these nuggets I learned from my coach Mary Morrissey on the power of gratitude. May they help you in leading yourself and your tribe with gratitude.

- Gratitude is not static.
- Gratitude is an open door to a happier, healthier, wealthier life.
- Gratitude is the frequency that is harmonious with abundance.
- The Power of Gratitude is in taking control of the direction of our own thinking, our own feeling and our own choosing, moment by moment. We often focus on what's missing or what seems wrong.
- Gratitude opens our awareness. We think differently when we're thinking from gratitude. When we live from gratitude, we see opportunities that were here all along, but we couldn't see them from the frequency of doubt, worry, fear, criticism or blame.
- Choose gratitude over complaint. It's necessary to cultivate the habit of being grateful and to give thanks continuously.

The last nuggets are from me.

- Start each day with gratitude. You have the power to change a life by exercising and expressing gratitude.
- Always remember, Gratitude leads to Grace.

THE BOOK ON GRATITUDE

Notes

Maria Duffy

---※---

Maria was born 70 years ago in Brierfield, near Burnley, in the northwest of England. After school, she chose to become a hairdresser and enjoyed the creativity in that field. After seven years, an opportunity presented itself to travel to and work on the island of Bermuda.

She liked the idea of a paradise island, and her course was set. In Bermuda, she met and married her husband, Charlie, and they had three children.

Maria switched to retail when she returned to work after the children were older. For the last eleven years, she created and has managed the Red Cross Thrift Shop near Hamilton.

She has loved seeing the world more than ever in these past few years. Twice she traveled to India and in September trekked to the Mount Everest Base Camp which required some training and endurance.

She still competes and wins in her age group with no plans to slow down!

Keep Going!

By Maria Duffy

"There are two lasting bequests we can give our children: One is roots, the other is wings."

— Hodding Carter, Jr.

Inspiration and Gratitude travel back and forth between mother and daughter and Flora and I are proof of that.

Seventy years ago, I was born in Brierfield, a small place near Burnley in the north-west of England. On leaving school I trained and qualified as a hairdresser. After working in the area for seven or eight years, I applied for a job on the island of Bermuda.

I figured that *sun, sea and sand* would suit me down to the ground. I am still here—forty-six years going so I guess I was right. And I am grateful I made the move.

While on the island, I met handsome Charlie in 1980 and it was love. We married and had three children in the next ten years: Joel, Flora, and Campbell in that order. Our boys, like Charlie and me, were very sporty. Joel's first love is soccer, which he played at the very highest level, including with the Bermuda National squad. Campbell took up competitive sailing, winning many local races and travelling overseas to compete in international regattas. His sailing exploits even made him a 'cover man' as an action photograph of him sailing was chosen to promote a men's after shave.

So, as a family we all participated in sports, including our little girl, Flora, who at the age of just eight told us she was going to win a medal at the Olympics.

> *"If you want to be the best, you have to do things that other people aren't willing to do."*
> — Michael Phelps

Flora started in the ranks of a swim club at seven years of age and soon after was training each Saturday morning with Tri-Hedz, a kids triathlon group. Like other parents do, Charlie and I would take Flora to swim and triathlon training sessions, where we both got inspired to assist in the kids training. We also did a little triathlon training ourselves whenever possible. As the song goes, *'Don't let the parade pass you by'* when it's so much more fun to participate. So, at the age of forty, I too started competing in triathlons, inspired by Flora.

For those unfamiliar with triathlon, it's three disciplines raced one after the other: swim, bike, run.

Flora won many, many races over her early years racing, and was slowly becoming known as someone to watch in the sport, keeping her Olympic dreams alive.

When Flora qualified for the 2012 London Olympics, excitement was high. Her goal was coming true. My husband and I traveled to be with her there and watch her race. The 1.5km swim course was at The Serpentine in Hyde Park, and Flora came out of the water well positioned in the race. She quickly transitioned on to the bike and got into a group in the middle of the pack. As she was negotiating a turn right outside Buckingham Palace, her bike hit a slick patch on the road, skidded and fell under her, sending Flora tumbling. There was a collective gasp from the spectators, and we held our breath and prayed for her safety, while we waited for news from that part of the course.

Fortunately, she was able to remount her bike and pedal towards the transition to the run and then the finish line. We were grateful our

THE BOOK ON GRATITUDE

Flora was not seriously injured, but of course her dream had been shattered and her feelings hurt.

That was a tough experience to come back from, and some thought it might be the end of her triathlon career. But not Flora. She vowed to keep going.

But there was another disappointment. Not long after that Olympic fall, she sustained a foot injury that required rest and recuperation for two years. So, no training or racing, but it did seem to refresh her mentally.

In 2020, Flora was given another opportunity to realise her gold medal dream, at the Tokyo Olympics. Fifty-five of the best women triathletes in the world were competing to stand on top of that podium. Flora among them. She was in a small group of half a dozen to exit the water first and took off on the 40km bike course in first place. In fact, she had both the fastest bike time, and then the fastest run time among all other competitors, led from the front, and romped home more than a minute ahead of her nearest rival.

Remarkably, Flora's dream had come true, and what's more, she had won Bermuda's first ever Olympic Gold Medal.

On returning to Bermuda, Flora received a heroine's welcome. She was met at the airport by a cavalcade of dignitaries and rode in a limousine very slowly to the capital of Hamilton, past her schools where children were cheering her excitedly from the sidewalks. She received the key to the city from the Mayor of Hamilton and met with the Premier of Bermuda.

She has also had a steep hill, part of a Bermuda triathlon course, renamed after her, the running track at the National Stadium is now known as the Flora Duffy Track, a suite at the toney Hamilton Princess & Beach Club is named the Flora Duffy Suite, and perhaps the biggest honour of all, she was made a Dame by Queen Elizabeth in the 2022 New Year's Honours list. Flora was recognised "for her exceptional contribution to sport in Bermuda over many years and for her outstanding achievements in triathlon, which include becoming the first and only person to ever win an Olympic gold medal for a British Overseas Territory.Her achievements also made Bermuda the smallest country, in terms of population, to win a gold medal at a Summer

Olympics. In addition to her Olympics win that year, Ms. Duffy also won the 2021 Xterra World Championship, the 2021 World Triathlon Championship Series Abu Dhabi and the Groupe Copley 2021 World Triathlon Championship Series Montreal."

Charlie and I were glowing and thrilled for her success.

How do I feel as the mother of this amazing daughter . . . Gratitude is in my heart always.

In November 2022, a World Triathlon Championship Series event was held in Bermuda and Flora and I both competed. Flora winning the ladies Elite race, and I my age category. Yes, we both won gold! Both Flora and I were grateful to be alive that day and participating as mother and daughter in our respective categories. And the Bermuda win positions Flora well to win a record breaking fourth World Triathlon Association title.

I think three things contributed to Flora's success: surrounding herself with supportive people, the right people who had knowledge and her best interests, and gratitude as she is overflowing with that — as are Charlie and me.

Remember to Keep Going!

Anecdote from Charlie Duffy

Two days before Charlie was due to give an acceptance speech "if" Flora won the Bermuda Athlete of the Year Award, he said, "I went grocery shopping at my local supermarket.

I was waiting to pay when the guy in front of me didn't have enough money for his total.

The guy started removing items and figuring out what he could afford. It was a slow day in the store so I said I'd pay the difference for him.'

When it was my turn with the cashier, she said, "That was very nice of you, Mr. Duffy." I said, "Maybe I'll play the lottery and be rewarded for my good deed."

The cashier said, "But Mr. Duffy, you already won the lottery the day your daughter was born."

And there was my acceptance speech!

THE BOOK ON GRATITUDE

Notes

JAN FRASER INSPIRED LIFE SERIES

Sharing
GRATITUDE

Lila M. Larson

---※---

Lila Larson is an international author, speaker, coach, mentor, Executive Coach, consultant and trainer with experience in Corporate, Private, Government, Education, Informational Technology, and Non-profit sectors. Her experience as a leader locally and nationally has resulted in bottom line results for her clients. Her current book *The Focused Leader* follows Lila's Leadership Philosophy: Clarity, Focus, Results.

She encourages clients who get 'Stuck' to take a deep breath in, hold it and then exhale while saying 'Up Until Now.' In doing so, they release the shadows, gremlins, whispers, and whatever has been keeping them from moving forward. By giving themselves permission to release all the past — they can focus on being fully present *'in the moment,'* to enjoy each day and look to the future they choose. What will it take for YOU to step into releasing the past, enjoying the present and creating the future you desire filled with Gratitude for who you are and what you have?

Contact
Website: www.lilalarsoninternational.com
Email: coachinglinks1@gmail.com

Gratitude is Timeless

By Lila M. Larson

"If you must look back, do so forgivingly. If you must look forward, do so prayerfully. However, the wisest thing you can do is be present IN the present ... Gratefully."

— Maya Angelou

It was late Friday afternoon the third week in October when the phone rang. The voice asked, "Do you still want to adopt a baby?" "Of course," I replied. "Well, Monday you can drive to Brandon, MB to pick up a baby boy and here is the address."

Frantically we prepared ourselves. This was the culmination of three years of tests, interviews, and a detailed home inspection. We arranged to borrow a vehicle which could have an infant seat installed (all we had was a converted school bus), friends gifted us a baby seat, relatives dropped off a bassinet and a crib was borrowed from a neighbor. A trip to Walmart for diapers, baby formula, sheets and crib bumpers, baby bottles, a bottle warmer, and baby blankets were quickly purchased. What did we need for the trip there and back? Who did we need to call and let know that our wait was over?

We stopped at a drugstore and purchased a newspaper for that day, for our records.

I pulled out the pages of questions we had prepared to gather information about the baby, his parents and their families, and as much health information and history as we could get. And armed with a notebook we left early Monday morning for the 2½ hour trip. We had not slept well the night before . . .

As we arrived at the Provincial Government Social Services Office, we found the right room and asked for the name of the person who had called us on Friday. While waiting for her to appear we saw at the end of the long row of cubicles a baby dressed in yellow in an infant seat on top of a desk at the end of that row. Was this OUR baby?

The woman who had called appeared and took us to a room with chairs and a couch. She reiterated her question from Friday — Were we still wanting a baby boy? Of course. She then said that the baby would be brought to us and we would have time to spend with him.

At that, there was a knock on the door and another woman came in carrying the baby dressed in yellow (that we had seen). They gave us a bottle of formula to feed him. As we reached for him, the two women left the room giving us time to hold, look at, speak to him (he was 7 weeks old), and he looked up at us with his bright blue eyes (and a bald head). We marveled at what a beautiful baby he was and how blessed we were to have him in our family. As we passed him back and forth between us, he was so alert and kept looking at us . . . (Wondering who we were? What did that mean for him?)

After an extended time, the social worker returned to the room. By then we had fed him, burped him and were holding him — our precious bundle of joy.

We were astounded as she asked, "So do you still want this baby boy? It's alright if you don't, your name will stay on the list until another baby boy comes up. You are not obligated to take this baby boy."

We looked at each other and then at her. "Of course, we want this baby boy and today!"

She replied that it had happened in the past that when the adopting parents actually saw their prospective baby, that they said no and were prepared to wait for the next baby.

That was incomprehensible to us — to say no to the precious baby boy. I tightened my arms about this bundle.

The social worker then proceeded to ask us numerous questions (we thought the past three years of questions had all been asked — wrong). Then, I pulled out my file of questions to gather information about the baby. We wanted to know his birth parents, grandparents, how the baby came to be, where his birth families lived, and their health information.

We learned that his birth parents were friends and lived on the Armed Services base near Carberry. The two teens (15 and 16) got along really well together and the parents were pleased, until she became pregnant. At that point the birth father's family moved away to another base. The birth mother's family was supportive and she carried the baby to birthing time. Even then, she was conflicted about keeping the baby or putting him up for adoption, so the baby was placed in a foster family until the court date when she was required to make a decision. This meant that until that court date that she could decide to keep the baby.

The court date was that Friday (when we had received the call) that she made the decision to place the baby for adoption and we were on the list as the first call.

The records were sealed until some point in the future, if or when either our son or we asked to make contact. At that point, we were not even thinking about that possibility.

As time passed, we were very protective of public announcements and photos, until the adoption waiting period had ended. We didn't want the birth parents to have any idea of where our son was or what he looked like.

Driving to the Winnipeg Adoption Office to sign the final papers was a trip filled with a mix of excitement and trepidation. Would she have changed her mind? Could he be taken away from us? What would we do if she had changed her mind?

The car seat was in the back seat and he was playing with his shoes, pulling at the laces. Until we arrived and parked the car, I did not realize that he only had one shoe on. The window beside him had been opened enough that I'm guessing he threw the shoe by the laces out the open window. We arrived in the office with a baby with only one shoe. The Social worker just laughed and suggested our life would have a series of unexpected events as he grew.

The final papers were signed (she had not changed her mind). I had brought the file of questions with me and was able to add more answers to that list of questions about his birth parents, their families and their health status. We stopped for ice cream to celebrate on the way back home.

What have I learned from this event?
- Life is filled with surprises.
- Gifts come in all shapes and sizes.
- People are there to offer support and encouragement.
- It's never too late to pursue dreams.
- God is good . . . All the time.

In the years that have followed I continue to be grateful:
- That this young mother had the courage to think of what was best for her baby.
- That she had not changed her mind when it was time for the final papers to be signed.
- That her family had continued to support her during her pregnancy and afterwards.
- That she had decided to make a career of assisting youngsters with disabilities.
- That my parents were supportive of us as we began our family with this precious baby boy.

He has been a source of joy and love over the years reminding me daily that gratitude is timeless.

Ode to Gratitude
by Lila M. Larson

Gratitude is an energy of your personality. Choose it.
Gratitude is a choice to make every day in every situation.
Gratitude seeks light
Gratitude seeks the positive
Gratitude seeks kindred spirits
Gratitude seeks solutions
Gratitude is a gift to be shared with others
Gratitude fills my soul
Gratitude AND hope are partners
Gratitude is a muscle that strengthens with each learning
Gratitude is called forth from our learnings
Gratitude replaces "being stuck"
Gratitude is kindness
Gratitude unleashes joy
Gratitude celebrates abundance
Gratitude is love
Gratitude is our dreams
Gratitude speaks MY truth
Gratitude lies in the spaces
Gratitude is unspoken or not
Gratitude is inside my heart
Gratitude is MY world
Gratitude is saying YES
Gratitude is between whispers
Gratitude is timeless

Myrto Mangrioti

Myrto, a #1 International Best-Selling Amazon author, is a Canfield Success Principles & Methodology Certified Trainer and a certified Deep Coach, Oola Life & Green Gap Coach.

Music and traveling have a special place in her heart. She spent 20 years working as a Production Assistant, organizing concerts all over the world. She decided to drop everything and founded Loving Living to pursue her passion for transforming the world, one person at a time.

Struggling with her "good girl" attitude all her life, she found peace by embracing it. Myrto created the "Yes-Girl Toolkit", to help other good girls discover their voice, stand up for themselves, and confidently ask for what they want. Watch out for her new book coming out soon!

Early morning, you can find her at the beach. She's vegan and loves nature. Meditation, yoga and cooking inspire and ground her.

She lives by one word: EMBRACE. Embrace yourself. Embrace the present moment. Embrace your life.

Contact
Website: www.loving-living.com

Activating the Law of Attraction with Gratitude

By Myrto Mangrioti

"Gratitude unlocks the fullness of life. It turns what we have into enough, and more. It turns denial into acceptance, chaos to order, confusion to clarity. It can turn a meal into a feast, a house into a home, a stranger into a friend."

— Melody Beattie

There was a time I was so depressed I couldn't find gratitude in anything! Nothing made me happy. Life was hard. I was working more than fifteen hours a day and my business was still losing money. I felt alone and unworthy. I was stressed all the time. No wonder I couldn't appreciate anything in my life.

Do you ever feel that the days pass, and you're a helpless puppet? Going through your day like a robot. That's how I felt. My days were uninspiring, stressful and almost identical. I woke up each morning, around five am, sat at my desk in my home office and worked on my computer, in my pajamas, for about four hours, writing and answering emails, planning my work day. I then showered, got dressed and went to the office around ten am, to take care of business. Trying to find solutions to daily problems as they were coming up: customers, staff relations, attitude issues, and product supplies. The most important was cash flow. Money was scarce which stressed and scared the hell out of me. It was a constant battle.

In the evening, I came back home around eight pm and crushed on the couch, too exhausted to even move. Watching anything on TV to take my mind off work-related problems. Excessively eating and drinking red wine to relax. Then, I went directly to bed, to start over the next day.

I worked most weekends too, to catch up on things I couldn't take care of while being in the office. There was always something to do. Attend exhibitions my company was taking part in or seminars we organized for our customers. I literally had managed to have no free time at all!

The worst part of it all was I didn't even like the business I was in! So even small wins I achieved didn't give me any satisfaction. Come to think of it, it's probably why I wasn't making any money! It took five years of this, for me to realize I was on the wrong path. I needed to start taking care of me. Living life. Enjoying life. Doing things I like.

I found help in self-development programs. I started following the instructions.

"Before you can ask for what you want in life, learn to appreciate and be grateful for what you already have!"

'What the hell are they talking about? My life is a mess! What's there to appreciate? Nothing.' This was my initial reaction. But I decided to go along with the suggestion. After all, they're the ones who are successful, and I'm the one struggling, so they must know something more than I do!

The Jar of Gratitude

During that period of my life, finding one thing to be grateful for each day was a struggle. One day, I saw on Facebook a post about something called the Jar of Gratitude. The idea is to have a big jar labeled "The Jar of Gratitude" and everyday write something you're grateful for on a piece of paper, and throw it in. When you're feeling down, you lift yourself up by reading what you've already written. I loved the concept!

I set up everything. I put my Jar of Gratitude, a post-it and a pen, on the table near the entrance of my house. My intention was to drop something in, every day when I returned from work. How hard could this be? Well, it turned out to be a difficult task! That's what depression does to you. Somedays I forced myself to write "I'm happy and grateful." Period. Not actually feeling it. One day I wrote "I'm grateful for my air-conditioning" . . . I guess it must have been a very hot day . . . Hahaha! Another, 'I'm grateful for my cats that bring me joy.' That was better! Slowly, finding things that brought me joy. That was more the spirit! Training myself to be grateful again.

What are You Looking Forward To, Today?

Another exercise I began doing each morning, in the shower, was to think of one thing I was looking forward to in my day. Again, in the beginning... nada! Nothing was coming to mind. My best answer was "Coming back home tonight to eat and watch Netflix with my cats!" It was a shocking realization! But what it did, was to push me to make changes. It also forced me to start looking for small pleasures during the day that made me happy and grateful. And it started working.

I learned there are always things in your day to love, appreciate, enjoy and be grateful for. All you have to do is look for them.

It's All About Mindset

It's all about mindset. You can choose to focus on all the bad stuff. What's not working, what's ugly or shabby. What annoys you, irritates you or makes you angry. What's broken or what makes you sad. On the other hand, you can be present and look around you for all the beautiful, ordinary or extraordinary things that are constantly surrounding you. You can turn your attention to the little stuff that brings you joy every day.

You may think, "How easy is it to change my mindset and my attitude? I've been like that all my life." Or, "I'm in the middle of a very bad situation." For starters, it's very important to be aware of it. Knowing and acknowledging something is wrong is the first step to fixing it. And I have good news. There's a cure. A proven method I've also tested with amazing results. It's an Affirmation. And it works like a charm!

Affirmations

An Affirmation is a statement you make about something you want in your life as if it has already occurred. Like it's already true. It's always stated in the present tense, in a positive way. And it's always about you. The sentence starts with "I'm happy and grateful now that . . . " and you complete it with whatever you wish you had in your life. It can be about anything.

You can use the affirmations for attitude shifting or specific things you want:

> *"I'm happy and grateful now that . . . "*
> *"I can enjoy precious time with my children"*
> *"I see the beauty in small things in my life"*
> *"I'm at my perfect weight"*
> *"I feel optimistic about my life"*
> *"I have all the free time I want . . ."*

Create your statements according to your needs. Anything that would be great for you. The key is to repeat the affirmation daily and to try and feel how it would be like, if that statement was true.

In the beginning, saying it may make you feel like an imposter, like you're lying to yourself. But that's the whole point. It feels this way because it's about something that needs change within you or in your life. As time goes by, the uneasiness will begin to fade away and you'll start to see the results manifesting in your life.

A word of caution. It doesn't work if it's about another person, for instance "I'm happy and grateful now that I'm married to Paul. Who, by the way, I've been in love with since forever, but is now happily married to Sue!" No, no, no! Don't go there! What you could say instead is "I'm happy and grateful now that I'm dating (or married to) the love of my life." Let the Affirmation do its magic. Be open to what it will bring.

I believe Affirmations work! I used them to get over my fear of public speaking. To my amazement and disbelief, I did! I'm grateful because now I can speak and lecture and help others overcome their blocks and experience life as best as they can. That's a story for another time.

The Light at the End of the Tunnel

Here is what happened to sad little me. Using gratitude, learning to appreciate what I already had, opening myself to new possibilities, I started seeing the light at the end of the tunnel. I realized that there's always some good in every moment, but we must be willing to find it. Slowly and steadily, I started changing my mindset. which reflected in my life. I switched careers, and I'm now doing something that I love: helping people find their way in life and enjoy it as much as possible.

As my life shifted, I began to look deep inside me to find answers. To find what makes me happy and how I can express myself. How can others experience me at my best. I defined my five core spiritual values and Gratitude is one of them. The others are Love, Acceptance, Authenticity and Playfulness.

I now try to live according to my core spiritual values and to embody them. I always ask myself, "Is what I'm feeling, doing, thinking, experiencing right now in sync with my core spiritual values?" This question grounds me and keeps me focused on being me. Being my authentic self, releases my creativity and makes me enjoy the moment. Enjoying the moment makes me grateful for it. Being grateful induces feelings of love and peace in me, which in turn brings me more of what I enjoy!

Attitude of Gratitude

That's why I created the "Today, I'm Happy and Grateful" series in my social media. Every day or so, I share one thing I'm grateful for and others can join me and share their thing. It's a constant reminder of what gratitude brings into my life, so that I never forget.

What I know now is that my life wasn't that bad. I allowed it to be like that in my mind. I forgot what it was all about. I needed to remind myself. It wasn't easy, but when I made the effort, the conscious choice, I put the Law of Attraction in motion. Things started shifting. The more focused on what I was grateful for and what made me happy, the better my life became.

The Law of Attraction

Like attracts like. That's the only rule of the Law of Attraction.

The more grateful you are the more things you find to be grateful for. The happier and more fulfilled your life will be. This is how the Law of Attraction works. Use it to your advantage!

Every day, ask yourself, "What brightens my day? What do I take for granted that I would miss if I didn't have? What am I grateful for?" Then, stand back and watch, as the Law of Attraction brings more of all these things to you.

Celebrate what you receive! Be grateful for it. Make it a never-ending cycle of acknowledgment, gratitude, attraction, joy and celebration.

Notes

Paddy Briggs

For over 20 years, Paddy Briggs has been a Practice Management Consultant & Trainer specializing in working with dentists and their teams. She combined her knowledge of business, and customer service philosophy to create and refine practical, effective strategies that assist dentists in growing their business and delivering the highest level of patient care.

In 2019 Paddy graduated with the Jack Canfield Group as a "Certified Transformational Coach and a Success Principles Trainer. Her focus now is coaching and empowering women in their business, career or their personal life. She inspires women to become all they were meant to be and to "live their best life".

Paddy lives on beautiful Vancouver Island in British Columbia, Canada steps away from the ocean. As much as she loves to travel, she is always so grateful to come home to her happy place on the beach.

Contact
Website: www.paddybriggs.ca

It's Never too Late

By Paddy Briggs

"Gratitude turns what we have into enough."

— Aesop

A few months ago, my daughter sent me a link from a local photographer. She was looking for 40 women over 40 years of age to photograph for a magazine she was publishing. My daughter said, "Mom, you need to do this!"

I started to laugh! "Are you kidding me? I'm in my 70's, and I'm sure she is looking for younger women." Let's face it, my first thought was 'I don't think I'm good enough to be in a magazine.'

In looking back, I realized I still had this limiting belief: 'I am not enough — I am not good enough — I am not attractive enough' which goes way back to when I was very young. I was a chubby little girl with an overbite that certainly was not attractive. In school I was teased about being fat and having buck teeth. Boys would say "Fatty Paddy, two by four — can't get through the bathroom door," and they would call me "Bucky, bucky beaver." This was the start of my image development as a young person. It was the story I was telling myself.

When I got to junior high school, I decided I wanted to lose some weight. My mom was very helpful. She always cut up veggies in the fridge *instead of chocolate chip cookies* which was my normal after school snack. Slowly, the weight started to come off, however, the image I had of myself didn't change. It's interesting how you retain your limiting beliefs. I believed my friends were always prettier, thinner, and more attractive than me! I used to cover up my feelings by laughing and making fun of myself.

Over the past few years, I have worked on my limiting belief 'I am not enough — I am not smart enough' regarding my career and in doing that I became certified as a Jack Canfield Transformational Coach and Trainer in his *Success Principles*. However, when my daughter sent me this link from Adrienne, the photographer, I realized I had not worked on my limiting image belief because I still thought — I didn't look good enough!

Something inside me said, 'email Adrienne and apply to be one of the women.' I DID that and after a phone call with her, I was ACCEPTED.

My photo shoot was scheduled. When I arrived, I felt an immediate connection with Adrienne. We had a great time, a lot of laughing, and I was totally relaxed. Sometime after the shoot Adrienne emailed me and asked me to be the *Cover Girl* for the magazine and that's not all — she then told me that I was the centerfold. I was shocked! Can you imagine a chubby little girl with buck teeth who is now in her 70's a cover girl and centerfold! Again, I laughed, however, I was filled with a great sense of humility and gratitude.

I had no idea how this would impact me, how this would change my whole thinking about myself. I thought about how I present myself, what made Adrienne choose me for the cover and centerfold. I realized it's *wonderful* to be enough. I could celebrate who I was. I could be happy with myself that I put out positive energy that encourages people . . . that is what I'm meant to be and do in my life.

You see, I could have missed out on this amazing opportunity all because of my limiting belief. Please don't underestimate yourself, no matter what our age we have so much to give.

There is nothing more exciting than to live your purpose and to be enough!

I am telling this story with gratitude because this was my breakthrough in my limiting image belief. I finally realized I am all I am supposed to be — I am enough . . . it took me a lot of years to break through this limiting image belief and I couldn't be more grateful!

As I look back on this experience, I realize I have so much to be grateful for. First, my daughter for believing in me and encouraging me to call Adrienne. Grateful for my health and energy at this age, grateful for each day that I wake up! I am grateful for Adrienne of Vital Image Photography who saw something in me that I couldn't see because of a limiting belief that I had carried for years. This belief has held me back, a belief that I wasn't enough.

We all have a story. We have limiting beliefs that hold us back from achieving our dreams and our goals. I tell my story to inspire women to love themselves no matter what age — live in gratitude — be grateful for who you are, your talents, your skills, your health, your energy, and your creativity. Smile more often, laugh more and let everyone see that beautiful face. Yes, it might have wrinkles, we've earned them. Never underestimate who you are and what you can do and celebrate when someone connects with you and sees something in you that you don't see yourself.

Let's teach our daughters and granddaughters to be grateful for who they are, love who they are for they are enough. Be grateful for who you are — you are so enough . . . you have a purpose. Don't let a limiting belief hold you back!

According to self-help author and blogger Mark Manson, *"Limiting beliefs are false beliefs that prevent us from pursing our goals and desires."*

I've learned it's never too late to breakthrough our beliefs that limit us. The most important key is learning to love yourself completely and to Live in Gratitude every day! ✺

Diane & Bob Palmer

Diane is a successful investor as well as co-author with her husband Bob of the Amazon #1 Bestseller, *Twist the Throttle to Fuel Your Success*, as well as a contributing author to the Amazon #1 International Bestseller, *The Book On Joy*.

Bob's roots come from the video production world where he has earned four Emmy awards as well as an International Monitor award for video editing as well as a Peabody Award.

Together they coach and put on workshops and trainings where they help others find their paths to success through their company, Palmer Motivation.

Contact
Website: www.palmermotivation.com

Grateful Start = Grateful Heart

By Diane & Bob Palmer

"Gratitude is the healthiest of all human emotions"

— Zig Ziglar

Gratitude — the practice of being thankful and grateful. Being thankful and grateful for the many things that are good, and sometimes even for the things that are not so good in your life. We say practice, because we truly believe we need to practice this for it to become a regular and constant part of our lives. It may sound simple, but that's not to say it's easy. In fact, sometimes it can be downright hard to be grateful, and even harder to be grateful on a regular basis.

You probably know somebody who has a heart of gratitude, grateful 99% of the time. These people are a treat to be around. They tend to rub off on others. When we're around them our troubles and our problems seem to be less than they were before. We feel lighter and more refreshed when we're around these people. We smile more and laugh just a bit harder. They make us feel better about life.

Gratitude is an amazing emotion. Both Bob and I love to focus on gratitude because we believe it turns us inward. It forces us to appreciate things and people and circumstances that otherwise, we might not stop and take note of. When you focus on gratitude and what you're grateful for, you see things from a different point of view. You start to acknowledge and appreciate the people you love, the things you have in your life, and often, you start to see and realize the person you are and who you've become.

We are Diane and Bob Palmer. Together, we own and operate Palmer Motivation, a personal development company. Bob is a Personal Development trainer and coach, and I do all the behind-the-scenes work that supports and runs our business. As Bob likes to say, "Diane is the wizard behind the curtain making all the things happen successfully out front."

We don't do a workshop, training, or coaching session without first taking time to ask each person in the group to acknowledge three things they are grateful for. We do this for a couple of reasons. One is that on any given day we're all surrounded by demands and expectations. Some are external and some internal. Often, these demands, and expectations will overtake our senses and we start to feel the pressures of life. We start the negative talk in our heads and start beating ourselves up for who knows what, that may have happened, or not happened in our past that we no longer have control over. This negative talk then stirs up negative emotions and before you know it, you're in a funk. By starting our sessions and trainings with gratitude, our participants focus on what they are grateful for and this turns their whole beings around, instantly putting smiles on their faces and lifting their spirits.

After they come up with three things, they are grateful for, we have them share those with someone else. The act of sharing helps cement this feeling of gratitude and thankfulness into their hearts. They're instantly feeling better about themselves and their environments. Now, the clients are better able to start working on their goals and situations. They are better equipped to come up with great and usable actions and strategies that will help them move forward.

Having an attitude of gratitude makes a huge difference on how you look at life and everything in it. We were in a training years ago when we first learned about this. It was amazing to both of us how fast our senses and emotions changed, just by thinking about the things in our life that we were grateful for.

In *The Book on Joy*, my chapter shared an idea we called our Joy Box. It captured our special moments throughout the year. We added notes and precious mementos, anything that had brought us joy and gratitude. There were no limits on what was collected, but we wanted things that we could use to treasure times that brought us special meaning. We would go through the box on New Year's Eve, and relive the tender moments of the past year with gratitude.

In fact, let's stop and do a quick exercise right now. Think of three things that you're grateful for in your life. OK, now either take a moment and write them on the inside cover of this book or make a note on your phone. Go ahead and do it now.

How do you feel now? Did you notice that little smile you had on your face when I asked that question? Amazing, isn't it? It's crazy how doing that simple task can change your thinking and how you feel in a short time.

Who knows what draws us together or toward someone more than another, but even as kids, both Bob and I continually paid attention to being grateful. That may have been the initial draw for both of us to each other. Who knows.

After doing this exercise on being grateful at the workshop years ago, we started putting gratitude into our daily routine. We do this for ourselves as well as teaching it to our clients. We have a routine that sets us up for success each day that starts with questions. Some have one-word answers and a couple of them have multiple word answers. The question that starts the whole list off is the question about gratitude. We like to start the day by asking ourselves the three things that we're grateful for. We do this because this sets us up in the proper frame of mind to take on the day.

If you don't have a routine that you start your day with, we suggest you create one. Both of us are huge believers in having routines because they help streamline many things in our lives. We develop our practices and habits to save us time and keep us safe. Take for instance, your use of knives in the kitchen. We develop routines and habits around using knives to keep us safe and not hurt ourselves.

After a short time, you will find that your morning routine will become a habit. And we think you'll agree, that having a habit of being grateful is an exceptional one to have.

We started this chapter by defining gratitude as the practice of being thankful and grateful. How often do you thank people in your life on a regular basis? Do you thank the grocery clerk, the barista at the coffee shop, the person that holds the door open for you, or the stranger that helps unexpectedly? Being grateful and being thankful makes a big difference in your life, and also in the lives of those around you. The point is, we don't think that we can ever be too thankful or too grateful in life. We encourage you to be aware of others trying to make your life better and be grateful for them every day.

It would be phenomenal, if at the end of our lives, when asked to say something about us, numerous people would agree that we were grateful for the things in our lives and thankful for everything and everyone.

That would be the best, a life well-lived with gratitude.

THE BOOK ON GRATITUDE

Notes

Maria Elena Laufs

Maria Elena Laufs is a university lecturer and Success Principles™ trainer. After spending 20 years in the world of international retail and fashion buying, she left it all behind for love before forging a new career in English as a Second Language teaching. After 10 years in a variety of lecture halls, she added personal development training to her repertoire.

Her aim in all of her work has always been to inspire confidence. From the magic of a flattering outfit, to the certainty of authentic communication in a foreign language and the power of a well-defined goal, the common thread is helping people to become the absolute best they can.

When not teaching or training, you'll find her attempting to master yoga poses, surfing clothing websites keeping abreast of the latest trends, or with her head stuck in some kind of personal development book. Born and bred in the UK, Maria Elena has lived and worked in a number of countries and is now happily living in Madrid, Spain.

Contact
Email: mariaelena@mariaelenalaufs.com

Take a Letter, Maria

By Maria Elena Laufs

"Feeling gratitude and not expressing it is like wrapping a present and not giving it."

— William Arthur Ward

I felt as if my legs had been kicked out from under me, both in the metaphorical and the literal sense. Despite having being warned that my dear auntie, Regina, no longer walked, I was totally unprepared for the complete and utter shock that I experienced when I walked into her kitchen and saw her in her wheelchair. A combination of the fact that she lived in a remote village in Galicia in the north west of Spain, together with strict COVID-19 travel restrictions, meant that it had been over two years since I had last seen her. Now, on the eve of her 90th birthday, she was a shadow of her former self. The chatty, amusing, strong-willed, at times bossy, woman I had known all my life had been replaced by someone barely able to talk, suffering from dementia and totally dependent on her live-in carer. All her joie de vivre had evaporated, leaving behind nothing but a sense of sadness and hopelessness. There have been very few times in my life when I have been rendered totally speechless, but this was one of them.

On the long drive back to my home in Madrid, I started to think about whether my auntie had any idea of how much she had meant to me over the years and how many treasured memories I have of her and our times together. As I am not naturally someone who expresses my feelings openly and explicitly for people to see, I would guess that she most likely didn't. Of course, I must have said thank you to her a million times for all the small things, those fleeting moments of gratitude that are spoken almost automatically, but expressing my deeply heartfelt gratitude for the accumulation of all those small things, for her being her and for being one of the cornerstones of my life is something that I had never done. The one thing I knew was that I didn't want to be expressing my profound gratitude in a eulogy at her funeral. I wanted her to know right now how important she had been and how grateful I was before it was too late. I knew what I had to do.

It was time to write a letter.

So, I sat down in front of my computer to start writing and came up with . . . absolutely nothing! Well, apart from a long list of reasons why I shouldn't do it. Regardless, I decided to do it anyway. I had never. written a letter like this before and didn't know where to begin. I felt awkward because I didn't know what to say and felt embarrassed at the thought of her reading it, not to mention, highly vulnerable, as well. I was putting my feelings on paper and making them concrete. This meant that there would be evidence and no going back. What's more, I also wasn't 100% sure that my auntie's reaction would be a positive one and, on top of everything, I had the added challenge of writing and expressing myself in Spanish, which is not my native language. At that moment in time, I would rather have undergone voluntary dental surgery than write that letter.

Brushing all my concerns aside, I decided that I had made a commitment to myself and would only regret not doing it. So, I shut my laptop, got a blank piece of paper and began to brainstorm. After an initially cumbersome start, I started to get into the groove. I replayed the scenes in my mind and made notes of the details; where exactly we went shopping, what we talked about, what the dress she made for me looked like and when she taught me to sew. As the recollections flowed, my angst disappeared and I went from squirming in discomfort to feeling positively enthused by the process. Finally, I had all the puzzle pieces. All that was left to do was put them together in a coherent text that conveyed the right message. Three typed pages later, my very first gratitude letter was complete. After adding some photos, I printed it out and put it in a beautiful card I had chosen especially for her. I posted it before I had time to change my mind.

My thoughts then turned to other people in my life who had been constants for many years and who may not know how much they are appreciated and treasured. People who have made my life better in a variety of ways. The trigger with my auntie had been the realization that she wouldn't be around forever, but the truth of the matter is that none of us know how many years we have left. As I reviewed my life and took a trip down memory lane, three names came to the fore.

The first was my friend and partner-in-crime of the past 50 years, Emma. Best friends since we met at primary school, there was an abundance of memories and gratitude waiting to be unearthed from the depths of my mind. From simply being my friend at school, to the lengthy Zoom chats we had every week during the strict European lockdown, and the countless examples of companionship and support in between. The hours spent chatting, fun experiences in foreign countries, thoughtful presents, secrets kept and of course, emotional support given (usually linked to some kind of man-induced turmoil). This was also the letter that scored highest on the 'feeling-embarrassed' scale. Emma knows me better than I know myself and she knows this isn't what I usually do. I chose to handwrite this one, which seemed to make the words flow more easily, both from my mind as well as physically over the paper using the smooth gel pen I had bought especially for the occasion. Seven pages later my second gratitude letter was ready. I popped it in the envelope with a carefully selected card that had a sheep on the front (because Emma loves sheep) and, as I didn't want to give myself the opportunity to have second thoughts, sealed it without reading it again. I was seeing her later that day and the thought of her opening it and reading it in front of me was absolutely mortifying. Giving her strict instructions not to open it until she was alone, I handed her the card.

Number two was my wonderful friend, Roseanne, who I had known for over 30 years. We met when we were both members of the management team in a branch of a fashion clothing chain. We bonded over the challenges of working for a rather demanding and exacting boss, which then led to a friendship characterized by numerous weekends together, lengthy phone calls, fun shopping trips, nightclubbing and experiments with some dubious clothing choices. However, my deepest gratitude was reserved for her character and how she has always been an inspirational model of a whole array of admirable qualities. She is the embodiment of positivity, resilience, dedication, loyalty and common sense. Putting pen to paper was easier with this one as I was becoming accustomed to writing straight from the heart, and feeling less embarrassed about it. Roseanne got a beautiful, glamorous, black and gold art deco style card which was the personification of her for me. Feeling relatively confident that it would be well-received, I took it straight to the post office.

My final letter was to my dear friend, former colleague and mentor, Jerry. By this time, I was on a roll and was positively relishing the process of writing these letters. This was a different relationship as Jerry had only been in my life for just over 20 years. We started working together when I was 34 and had just started a new job in the glamorous world of fashion buying. He is the epitome of integrity and professionalism, and my gratitude to him covered an array of both business and personal skills, including effective business communication, negotiating and how to spot a best seller. There were also numerous funny moments and hours spent chatting, which continue to this day. He has earned my eternal gratitude for being instrumental, if not borderline Machiavellian, in me marrying the love of my life. Jerry is quintessentially British, so I opted for a regal purple card with gold writing for him. Not without some uncertainty about how it would be perceived by him, I sent the letter on its way to England.

The process of writing my four gratitude letters has made me appreciate and value the people in my life even more and, most importantly, reflect upon what it is exactly that I value them for. As soon as you start to focus on gratitude, you notice more things to be grateful for. With each person, I started off with a blank piece of pa-

THE BOOK ON GRATITUDE

per and ended up with a waterfall of gratitude. However, the feelings of gratitude and happiness were tinged with an element of sadness. I don't know how much longer my auntie will still be here, and those three friends all live in a different country from me.

And what happened when the letters reached their destinations? How did my auntie Regina, Emma, Roseanne and Jerry react when they read them?

Regina's carer read the letter to her and told me it had made her extremely happy. She could remember all the events I wrote about, and even added additional details, such as how she had stayed up all night sewing the dress for me to wear to the races at Ascot. I didn't know that, and it only served to magnify my gratitude. She spent a lot of time quietly looking at the letter and the photos. It did also prompt some sadness, as it had in me, with the realization that those moments in time have passed and we are in different places now.

Emma left me hanging for an agonizing two days. As you can imagine, this immediately played to my fear of a negative reaction to what I had written. It turns out that it wasn't intentional and she had simply put the letter in the depths of her cavernous handbag and forgotten about it. When she finally dug it out, she loved it. As well as being a reminder of a lifetime of shared experiences, knowing how excruciating it must have been for me to write also gave her something to chuckle about.

Roseanne's reaction was simple. She cried. Tears of happiness, I'm presuming.

Jerry was flooded with emotions, both happy and sad. Gratitude and joy for the tangible expression of appreciation he had received. Regret for the people in his life who he had not acknowledged and were now no longer here.

As you have been reading this, my wish is that it has prompted you to think about someone in your life who you are thankful for, and ask yourself if he or she knows. If there is a shred of doubt in your mind, give them the gift of gratitude.

Take a letter, dear Reader.

Bernadette Ridge

❋

Bernadette is originally from Ireland and now lives on Spinnaker Island, close to Boston, MA. She is a former teacher with a B. Ed. Degree, and a seasoned Workforce Engagement software solutions specialist. Her passion is to help people live their best, most joyful, lives. She is certified in Strategic Intervention coaching, Miracle-Minded Coaching, the Barrett Values System Leadership & Coaching, as a Trainer in The Success Principles, Positive Psychology, Infinite Possibilities, Feminine Power, Robbins-Madanes and Somatic Breathwork, amongst others. She is also co-author in the Jan Fraser Life-Inspired book series and is training for a TEDx talk.

Bernadette is currently establishing herself as a Holistic Life Coach, author, speaker and Purposepreneur, leveraging different modalities including spirituality, physical and metaphysical transformations. She is a member of the Young Living (Essential Oils) and the World Happiness Community organizations, in addition to a powerful optimal health program.

Contact
Website (coming soon): www.bernadetteridge.com
Email: bernadette.ridge@gmail.com

Gratitude for My Like Minded Tribe

By Bernadette Ridge

"At times, our own light goes out and is rekindled by a spark from another person. Each of us has cause to think with deep gratitude of those who have lighted the flame within us."

— Albert Schweitzer

There could not be a more perfect day to be writing about gratitude than today, September 21, 2022, World Gratitude Day. I watched two great films, i.e., "Gratitude Revealed", by Louie Schwartzberg, and "It's a Wonderful Life," (1946) starring James Stewart as George Bailey. The latter really struck me because I lost my job on September 6th, along with hundreds of my colleagues, including most of the team I had worked closely with for three years. As I thought through the implications, I realized I was less focused on the fact that I would have no income or benefits after month end, and more so on how much I would miss my colleagues and friends.

To suggest "It's a Wonderful Life" to a person dealing with unemployment or loss of a loved one could be considered insensitive, but a self-empowerment technique known as the "George Bailey Effect" can generate psychological strength and increase positive emotions that are very helpful for facing what must be faced. In simple terms, the technique is to pick a person, place or event in your life that brings you joy and satisfaction, and then consider the various ways it might never have happened. Then, imagine your life without that person/place/event. I am now contemplating my own life without the security of a job and how we allow ourselves to become defined by what we "do" for a living. Although it's daunting, I realize that who I **am**, and what I choose to **be**, is more important to me now than finding another job.

A Course in Miracles says that a miracle is but a shift in perception, and the "Imagine if . . ." perspective allows for even traumatic events to be viewed through the lens of things happening *for* us, not *to* us, if we are willing to be grateful for our aliveness and those around us who love us, support us, lift us up and encourage us.

Mike Dooley speaks about "Thoughts become Things," and Melody Beattie reminds us that "Gratitude makes sense of our past, brings peace for today, and creates a vision for tomorrow."

Never has this been more meaningful than now in my personal world, as I think back to previous job losses, two divorces in two different countries, my brother's suicide, my youngest sister's recent cancer diagnosis, and other life-changing events. I realize that, by choosing peace and love, over fear, nothing bad happens. As a matter of fact, I went on to even happier places in life. And so, now, having allowed myself some personal time to reflect upon my thoughts and feelings about my future, I find myself thrilled at the prospect of not going back to "corporate America" and doing something I have been talking about for years. I want to help people become, to **be**, the best version of themselves, and if they are not sure what that looks like, well, let us figure it out together. I am transforming myself, once again, in my late 50's, and living my purpose as a holistic life coach, author, speaker and purposepreneur. I have the personal life experiences and the training to impact another human being in a positive way, which is the most fulfilling, joyful, and reciprocal experience I can imagine.

As for gratitude of those who light a flame within us, my "tribe" as

THE BOOK ON GRATITUDE

I call them, it is incredible what happens when you take steps in the direction of your dreams, who shows up, when and how. I hope you have already experienced much of that in your own lives already, but it truly never ceases to amaze me. After a day of wallowing, I shifted my energy and started to daydream about my next transition. Within a mere two-week timeline, I had done a TV interview about *The Book on Transformation*, spoken with three well-established coaches who are happy to guide me through practical steps, have two clients who asked if they could be the first to work with me, have three testimonials, a friend who will help with the website creation, and the full support of my friends and family. Most importantly, my intuition tells me I am on the right path, and I am grateful for the trust I now have in myself. That was not always the case.

The Universe/God/Angels, whatever higher power we believe in, always wants each of us to be in the flow of the joy that is our destiny. If you or I did not exist in this world, a lot of amazing things would never have happened, or would not happen in the future.

We are one collective consciousness, all inter-connected, and we each serve a unique purpose in making our world a joyous experience for all. This may sound lofty, but we each have the power to create joy for ourselves in a moment, or for another person, and those vibrations affect everything around us. This, in fact, is the only way world peace can ever be realized.

In the words of Marianne Williamson, "There is a new world struggling to be born, and all of us are called to be its midwives. To affect real change in our lives, we must alter perspective and take action. When we make this kind of intentional change, we can impact not only our own lives, but the world around us as well."

If ever there was a time to stand for something bigger than ourselves, it's now. We need an era of new beginnings, and a commitment to fundamental change, which includes inner as well as outer changes. As Martin Luther King Jr. once said, "Our goal is to create a beloved community, and this will require a qualitative change in our souls as well as a quantitative change in our lives."

It is so tempting to wallow in cynicism, desperation, hopelessness and anger, in these times particularly, but that is exactly what we must reject. We have a choice to make — to either be taken down by the undertow of current events or make a commitment to ourselves that in whatever way possible, we will be agents of change. We must "get into the solution." Sometimes, we don't exactly know how we might do that, but there is a power in knowing that we are committed to doing it. That's how we need to see transforming the world. We just need to be receptive enough, and available enough — and in our better hours, courageous enough — to consistently show up for the task. The path unfolds when we are willing to walk it.

The only choices now, really, are to either give up or to look up. To take the route of pathology or the route of enlightenment. To give in to fear, or to give it up for love.

There was an article about how little chickens know when it's time to hatch. A noxious gas begins to fill the inside of the eggshell, and they have to get out in order to survive. They are literally dying to be born. Precisely when it's time, the mother hen instinctively knows to tap on the eggshell from the outside, signaling to the babies where to break through to the other side. This is a good analogy for humans; we are literally dying to be born into something new. We are recreating ourselves, and thus, the world.

There are people who have deliberately removed themselves from my world. After experiencing the loss, different energy forces — our angels on earth — our 'tribe' — fill any voids, and we realize that it all happens for a reason. We can only see this clearly when we awaken to our soul's spirit, focus on gratitude, practice forgiveness, deepen our faith in ourselves and in the divine plan.

I have a neighbor and dear friend on Spinnaker Island. We spoke recently when she shared with me that she was going through various health challenges. Both being as spiritual as we are, we talked at a very deep, authentic level. I found myself saying something to her, intuitively, that even took me by surprise, and I received two text messages from her the next day. She told me that she had experienced two breakthrough moments, as she reflected on my observation about her being "blocked", and she ended her text with these words:

... *"I am crying because I'm finally consciously aware of my body, mind and spirit, and how it is all connected. I am a healer and I'm learning to heal me. As I said yesterday, being with you was the best meeting I've ever had with God. You said, I deserve easy and fun days. Much gratitude and love."*

Another relatively new and very dear friend shared his thoughts on our souls. *"Mystics know all about such realities, as well as Irish folks like ourselves, who still believe deeply in spirits, fairies and the holy angels that console us in the very dark and anguished hours."*

We never know who and how we are impacting by our words and actions, and at what level. By being totally present and open-hearted with another human being, that level of connection is transformative in some way.

I have also been thinking a lot about aging these days. I'm intrigued by Ralph Waldo Emerson's line, *"As I age, my beauty steals inward."*

Even though I have less physical energy than I once did, I feel like some level of power within myself is actually just revving up. I have a strong feeling that this particular chapter of my life is not supposed to be a diminishment, but rather a fulfilment of all the lessons learned up until now. Much like everyone else I know who has reached 50 and beyond, I am often bewildered by all the available aids to aging well. From my memory to daily energy levels, I have found ways to offset the stereotypical areas of decline. I am grateful for all the physical and spiritual ways I have discovered to help me age in a joyful way.

To the tribe of fellow co-authors all over the world, I am so grateful to know you and be on this journey with you all. To the readers of this chapter and the entire Book on Gratitude, I pray you will be impacted positively and encouraged by our stories, bringing more gratitude, transformation and joy into your own lives. You deserve it.

I will finish with an excerpt from a poem by one of my favorite human beings and close relative, Mike Lally, whose message for us is profound. I hope it resonates with you and inspires gratitude every day.

JAN FRASER INSPIRED LIFE SERIES

Try a little kindness, allow a gleam of hope,
Open up your hearts; together we can cope.
With peaceful co-existance we could be so far ahead.
Who cares about your political persuasion, if your heart is dead.
Now I must speak of LOVE — the cohesive force,
That, and that alone, can get us back on course.
We have just gone through the Winter, Spring is here at hand,
Let joy prevail within your hearts and Peace throughout our Land.

The Sea of Tranquility — My Amalgam — Mike Lally — 1/11/2021

Notes

Helen Holton

Dr. Helen Holton is a recovering elected official after 20+ years of service to Baltimore City. She reimagined life and leadership into a new reality. Today, she delivers earned expertise as a professional executive and leadership coach, trainer, speaker, and award-winning author. An interculturalist who brings perspective to local issues with global impact. Influenced by the intersections of race, gender, political power, and privilege guide her work with leaders (executives, entrepreneurs, and emerging). Credentialed and certified, she builds bridges to break down barriers across diverse industries, sectors, and people. Living an authentic life, she speaks truth to power and brings light into dark spaces. Anchored by faith in God drives her work toward greater inclusion, diversity, equity, and belonging. Dr. Helen enjoys travel, golf, spa treatments, and socializing with family and friends. Grace, Gratitude, and Resilience keep her focused and aligned with her purpose, passion, and calling to coach leaders to be better leaders.

Contact
Website: www.drhelenholton.com
Email: engage@drhelenholton.com

Resilience, Grace & Gratitude Saved My Life

By Helen Holton

"I have been sustained throughout my life by three saving graces — my family, my friends, and a faith in the power of resilience and hope."

— Elizabeth Edwards

Life is a continual journey of connections to help you evolve and grow into living a life full of joy, hope, peace, and gratitude. Gratitude is not an automatic given just because you're living. Disappointments and detours in life happen all the time and being grateful for them is usually not the first thing that comes to mind. Have you ever found yourself asking, "Why me? What did I do to deserve this?" The "this" is often the unexplained challenge, difficulty, or derailment life presents to you. I can imagine how you feel. I've asked myself the same questions . . . and some are still unanswered.

Life's not always easy or pleasant, and the experiences of your life don't always have answers, at least not the ones you want to hear. The ups and downs, triumphs and defeats, and everything else in between we live through can sometimes make you feel like you want to just stop and get off the merry-go-round of misery, disappointments, and broken dreams. Gratitude is the balm that can soothe the pains and heal the hurts of life. Even those that may seem too great to bear or never go away.

When you wake up to the dawn of a new day is a blessing. If you have a roof overhead, a warm bed to sleep in, and food to eat, you are blessed. Do you live with daily aches and pains to remind you of how blessed you are, even when they interfere with living the way you think you should be? Have you ever experienced something awful that changed your life forever? Interrupted the dreams and plans you had for your life? I have.

Resilience taught me to survive what seemed to be the end of my life. How to find the courage and strength to face painful, difficult, and unexplainable realities. Gratitude is a life force that opens you to new perspectives and ways of being. Gratitude teaches you to see and live in the silver lining of the clouds in your life. When you encounter traumatic life-changing experiences that come out of nowhere, it's gratitude that elevates you to a higher plain. It opens the path that leads your life into the overflow of daily blessings. A spirit of gratitude helps you live brighter days, even when the sun is not shining.

A bump on my arm the size of a pea warranted a visit to the doctor's office. It was a strange protruding addition I never really noticed until I noticed. As a healthy young woman advancing professional pursuits, this needed to be addressed and resolved. The doctor's visit to assess, address and fix was the beginning of the darkest period of my life. A physical abnormality led to a joint consultation between two physicians, an internist, and a dermatologist. They put their heads together to treat the problem and solve it with a cure.

Treatment began with an exam workup and a couple of biopsies to appropriately diagnose the problem. The outcome led to a few failed remedies, followed by shock therapy. A regimen of prednisone, a steroid drug, to shock my system and stop the spread throughout my body. The prescribed protocol was to ramp up to a very high dosage and back down in a short period of time, ten days. If you don't know about prednisone, by all accounts, it's a life-saving drug used for a multitude of seasonal and chronic health conditions. In my case, it created a condition that changed my life forever.

The ten days spent on prednisone are as memorable today as it was more than 30 years ago. In ten days, I'd gained ten pounds eating anything and everything I could get my hands on. My joints creaked, and I could hear and feel them throughout my body. The first warning sign was an acute attack of pain in my left hip that interrupted my ability to walk. Unable to get authorization to the Emergency Room while out of town, I popped a couple of Tylenol and cried myself to sleep. I knew something wasn't right and that the prednisone had something to do with it. It didn't agree with my body. Waking up hours later was like having a bad dream about something that had never occurred. Have you ever felt that way about something you wanted to deny as being real?

After the ten-day regimen life returned to a pre-prednisone state. No more insatiable appetite, no more squeaking, creaking joints; the ten pounds went away, and after six months of monitoring, the case was closed, and all was well. The nightmare was over, and life returned to normal. Have you ever been knocked down by life and you got back up to keep moving forward? Only to be knocked-out with a one, two punch followed by a ten count. It can leave you with a memory to last a lifetime.

Two years after the cure, the side effect reaction from the prednisone returned on Christmas Day. Attending the annual Christmas Brunch at Dad's house was always a fun gathering. All the festivities of the holiday, the tree trimmed with lights and ornaments, gifts underneath for family and friends, aromas of cinnamon potpourri filled the air; plenty of food, hot cider, eggnog, and holiday cocktails. Children in the basement playing with toys, adults upstairs catching up on life, laughing, eating, and having fun.

After sitting for a while with an empty glass, I decided it was time to get up for a refill of refreshments. I stood up and immediately fell back into my seat. There it was again. The prednisone. My left hip. The pain that caused my inability to walk was back again. It was no accident. I knew in my gut even with all the attempts to dismiss the truth; lightning had struck the same place twice. I remained seated, hoping, wishing, and praying that the next attempt to stand up would prove to be normal. It wasn't. I couldn't walk...again. Gripped with flashback memories, I summoned Dad's attention, who ironically was with me when the first attack of pain occurred.

It was Christmas Day, and although I was home, there wasn't anyone to give me authorization to go to the ER. It was a memorable Christmas for all the wrong reasons. Cutting the celebration short, using crutches for mobility, and being driven home to repeat the nightmare of two years earlier was not the ending in mind. A couple of Tylenol and the living room sofa is where slumber overtook the overwhelm of the unknowing. It was a scary déjà vu moment.

In the dawn of a new day, I was filled with a flurry of emotions ranging from confusion to fear, anger to blame, and defeat to despair. Like before, the pain and disability of the day before were more confusing because this time there was an absence of active prednisone in my system. It was an eerie suspicion that the damage had begun years earlier when prednisone was prescribed by doctors as the "fix," the cure to solve my problem.

From 1988 to 1991 I lived in pain 24/7, walking on canes and crutches, living on disability income from my job, and taking prescription opioids to address deep pain within that never went away. The turnaround breakthrough happened on January 10, 1991, in post-op recovery after my first total hip replacement. Laying with tubes, hoses, pumps, and IVs as I awakened, groggy from anesthesia, the first conscious thought was that the deep, nagging pain within was gone. The light at the end of a long dark tunnel was visible. It brought tears of joy and gratitude.

Life is full of twists and turns, hopes and fears, victories and defeats. Resilience isn't something we're born with; it's something we build throughout our lives. When you consciously connect with the power of resilience, it's a game changer. Resilience is a power that helps you persevere and push through the upsets of your life to pursue what you want for your life. It teaches you how to live strong on purpose with power.

When you build resilience, it keeps you from checking out of the game of life. Gratitude elevates your life and empowers you to play full out in your life. It keeps you humble and grateful for all things great and small within and beyond ordinary living. Gratitude fills you with indescribable joy, hope, and optimism for the here and now and what's next to come.

Monday, October 12, 2015, I had hip surgery #7. I went in without pain and have lived in pain every day since. Some days are better than others, and I've learned to count every day as a gift. Having endured multiple hip surgeries and still walking, most of the time unassisted, on my own two feet is nothing short of God's grace and the power of resilience and gratitude.

In the third quarter of life, as a woman of deep faith, I love God more than anything, without reservation and unapologetically. This wasn't always my story or truth; however, today it is. What began as a response to a health abnormality transitioned into multiple hip surgeries that changed my life forever. I'm grateful for every one of them. God's grace awakened the power of resilience and the priceless value of deep abiding gratitude. The best book in my life is the Holy Bible and 1 Thessalonians 5:16, 18 reminds me to "Rejoice always, give thanks in all circumstances . . ."

If you learn to give thanks for the good, the bad, and the indifferent experiences, it will transform your life into one filled with unimaginable blessings. Fill your cup with gratitude, and it will never be empty. Open the window of your soul for your countenance to shine from the inside of you into a world that needs to see and feel more joy, peace, hope, and love.

> "Rejoice always and give thanks in all circumstances."
> Amen. Asé.

THE BOOK ON GRATITUDE

Our Invitation to You

We honor you for investing in yourself by reading, receiving and feeling our love through our stories of how gratitude has touched our lives for good.

We hope you feel connected and share in our intention to Heal the World with Gratitude.

Create opportunities in your life, your community and your world to share Gratitude and to receive it gracefully.

Ask questions or request information on writing a chapter in our upcoming Inspired Life Series book: *The Book on Abundance*.

Attend a virtual or live Writer Retreat, or inspire others with pure Gratitude Essential Oil . . . reach out to us at info@bookongratitude.com.

Stay in touch with our Inspired Team at www.bookongratitude.com

With your help . . . We are "Healing the World with Gratitude"

Love,

Jan

Made in the USA
Columbia, SC
07 January 2023

75118195R00124